Half-Baked Gourmet™

PARTLY HOMEMADE TOTALLY DELICIOUS

DESSERTS

200 Quick-and-Easy Recipes for
Pastries, Pies, Cakes, and Cookies

Tamara Holt

A ROUNDTABLE PRESS BOOK

HPBOOKS

Most HPBooks are available at special quantity discounts for bulk purchases for sales promotions, premiums, fund-raising, or educational use. Special books, or book excerpts, can also be created to fit specific needs.

For details, write: Special Markets, The Berkley Publishing Group, 375 Hudson Street, New York, NY 10014

Notice: The recipes in this book are to be followed exactly as written. Neither the publisher nor the author is responsible for your specific health or allergy needs that may require medical supervision, or for any adverse reactions to the recipes contained in this book.

HPBooks
Published by The Berkley Publishing Group
A division of Penguin Group (USA) Inc.
375 Hudson Street
New York, New York 10014

Copyright © 2004 Roundtable Press, Inc.
Design: Charles Kreloff
Illustrations: Tony Persiani
Cover photograph © Foodpix/Mary Ellen Bartley

Roundtable Press, Inc.
Directors: Julie Merberg, Marsha Melnick
Executive Editor: Patty Brown
Editor: Sara Newberry
Production Editor: John Glenn
www.roundtablepressinc.com

All rights reserved. No part of this book may be reproduced, scanned, or distributed in any printed or electronic for without permission. Please do not participate in or encourage piracy of copyrighted materials in violation of the author's rights. Purchase only authorized editions.

First edition: September 2004

This book has been cataloged with the Library of Congress.
ISBN 1-55788-434-X
Printed and bound in China

10 9 8 7 6 5 4 3 2 1

Contents

There's nothing better than homemade dessert, and the best desserts are those you serve on a regular day, just to add a touch of sweetness at the end of a meal. Since dessert is, by definition, a treat, it should be easy to make.

In this book, ingredients such as cake mixes, refrigerated doughs, and prepared cakes take the work out of dessert-making. Many of the ingredients can be kept on hand, which cuts down on shopping time. Fewer ingredients means less measuring, which leads to less mess—so there's less clean-up time. So when you want to prepare a sweet treat, open the cabinets and see what you have on hand. Chances are, you'll have all the makings for a fantastic homemade dessert.

Half-Baked Gourmet: Desserts is ideal for busy parents who want to treat their families to something special at the end of a meal. It's for people who appreciate homemade treats but don't have the know-how or equipment to make everything from scratch. It's also a perfect way to teach children to appreciate the kitchen and cook for themselves. The recipes are easy, quick, and totally delicious.

INGREDIENTS

For the recipes in this book, I have limited the number of ingredients as well as those that need measuring to a bare minimum.

Since there are fewer ingredients, each one should be of the highest quality available.

Trouble deciding which brand to buy? Go for one with all natural ingredients. In the following guide, I'll fill you in on those that I use.

JAMS/SPREADS

A wide range of products exists in the jams and jellies section of your supermarket. **Fruit spreads** and **spreadable fruit** have the thickest consistency and can be used interchangeably. **Preserves** are made with whole or large pieces of fruit and usually still have seeds. **Jellies** don't have any fruit chunks. **Squeezable fruit** and **pourable fruit** are thinned to the consistency of a sauce and can be used in place of one another.

The less-common items from the jam and jelly department are **ginger preserves**, **lemon curd** (both commonly found under the label Wilkin & Sons Ltd.), and **Nutella,** a chocolate hazelnut spread. If they're not available at the supermarket, head for the closest gourmet store or find them online.

TOPPINGS

Ice cream toppings are useful step-saving ingredients. Smucker's® toppings are available in most supermarkets. For hot fudge, though, I prefer Hershey's®. **Dulce de leche** (milk caramel spread) was originally imported from South America, but is now produced in North America as well. I tested the recipes for this book with Magnolia® brand, which is not as thick as the imported ones. **Whole-stem ginger in syrup** is sold by Rafetto® and is available in gourmet shops. Store these toppings in the pantry until you use them. Once opened, they will last indefinitely in the fridge.

FROZEN JUICE CONCENTRATES

Frozen juice and drink concentrates are a great way to get intense fruit flavor. After opening, refreeze them in the smallest container you can find. Look for all-natural brands such as Minute Maid® Premium all-natural lemonade and limeade concentrates.

PREPARED COOKIES, CAKES, & BREADS

You will find many prepared cookies, cakes, and breads in this book—they are perfect bases for desserts. **Savoiardi biscuits** are crisp ladyfingers, most often used to make tiramisù. Look for them rather than the soft ladyfingers that you might see at the supermarket. The brand I prefer to use is Balocco. Lazzaroni® **amaretti di Saronno cookies** are easy to find in any Italian specialty or gourmet market. When you find them, buy extra and keep them on hand for the future.

The best meringue cookies that I've found come from Miss Meringue®. When I refer to **chocolate wafer cookies,** I mean the thin Nabisco Famous® chocolate wafers—they're excellent in recipes, but I can't resist them for snacking. For prepared cakes, I like Entenmann's®.

PUDDINGS AND GELATINS

Unless making the pudding is part of a recipe, you can use any prepared pudding. My favorite is Kozy Shack®. If you decide to make the pudding yourself, use the cook-and-serve variety—it's far superior to instant. **Unflavored gelatin** is sold by Knox®. Goya® flan mix will probably be found with the Hispanic foods, while Jell-O® flan mix will be with the puddings. They are different, and I use both brands in the recipes.

BOXED MIXES

I have limited the flavors of cake mixes to just a few. By adding flavor to a simple cake mix—by using orange juice instead of water, for example, you get fresh orange flavor that you wouldn't in an orange-flavored cake mix.

I use cake mixes without "pudding in the mix" and I like Duncan Hines® mixes. Duncan Hines chewy fudge is my favorite brownie mix and the one that I tested the recipes with.

For cookie mixes, I use Betty Crocker®.

REFRIGERATED AND FROZEN DOUGHS

Refrigerated cookie doughs can be transformed into fancy cookies, crusts, and bars. Pillsbury® makes a soft, puffy cookie; Nestlé® a flatter, crisper cookie. I prefer Pillsbury for these recipes; I find that it is more versatile. These doughs can be frozen and defrosted in the fridge before use.

Pillsbury® refrigerated pie crust is already mixed, rolled, and cut into rounds. It makes pie and pastry making, well, easier than pie.

For **frozen puff pastry,** I use Pepperidge Farm®. Be sure that it is completely defrosted before you start or the sheets will crack when you unfold them. If they crack, overlap the edges and roll lightly with a rolling pin.

Phyllo dough (also spelled **fillo**), is much easier to use than you might think. The trick to working with phyllo is to keep it from drying out. Keep the sheets covered with plastic wrap and a damp towel as you work.

CHOCOLATE

I mostly call for semisweet chocolate chips—they melt fast and are easy to measure. When you open a bag, put whatever you don't use in a sealable plastic bag and store it in a cool place.

NUTS

Pre-chopped nuts make cooking super-easy. Store them in the freezer in sealable plastic bags. There's no need to defrost them before use. Just remember to taste them before adding them to any recipe to make sure they aren't rancid.

FRUIT

Frozen berries are fantastic. Buy them by the bag, or, if you live where they are plentiful in season, you can freeze your own. Spread them in a single layer on a cookie sheet and freeze them solid. Transfer the frozen berries to a sealable plastic freezer bag. They will keep for ten months to a year.

Canned fruit shouldn't replace fresh in your diet, but in recipes it's fine. I tend not to bother using the "light" versions.

Dried fruit should be stored in an airtight container in a cool place or in the freezer.

A FEW ODD INGREDIENTS

When I refer to **almond paste,** I don't mean marzipan. You can find Solo® pure almond paste with the pie fillings in your grocery's baking section. It has a bit less sugar than marzipan, so if marzipan is all you can find, go ahead and use it, but reduce the sugar in the recipe by a tablespoon or so.

Chestnut spread is a sweetened chestnut purée. Don't buy plain chestnut purée: it is not sweetened. The spread is available in gourmet stores or online.

Coconut milk and **cream of coconut** are two different things. Coconut milk is thin, like water, and not sweetened. Cream of coconut is thicker, like a syrup, and is sweetened. They are available in the Hispanic or Asian foods sections of the supermarket.

Almond syrup is usually found in the beverage section of the supermarket and is usually made by Torani® or Monin®. If you can't find it, go to a specialty coffee or food retailer or check online. Try a shot of it in your coffee for a special treat.

EQUIPMENT AND TECHNIQUES

Cooking isn't fun when you become frustrated, don't have the necessary equipment, or don't understand a recipe. For the recipes in this book, you'll need basic equipment and to know how to use it—muffin tins, baking sheets, cake pans, measuring cups (liquid and dry), an electric mixer, and a food processor.

The techniques are also simple—mostly stirring, spreading, and sprinkling. The best thing about desserts is that even if a recipe doesn't come out perfectly, the result is usually yummy nonetheless. The only way a recipe can totally fail is if the oven is not the right temperature. Nearly every oven is off by a few degrees, but some are off by a lot—enough to ruin your recipe (and your day). So get an oven thermometer and check it before you bake anything.

You will also notice that many recipes direct you to look for signs of doneness, rather than just depending on a timer—"Bake until puffed and golden, 25 to 30 minutes," for example. The most important word in that sentence is "until." A slight difference in temperature, of the oven, your room, or the ingredients you started with can have an impact. Use the time as a guideline, but if it's "puffed and golden" at 23 minutes or not until 32 minutes, take it out then.

When using cake mixes, pay particular attention to oven temperature and equipment. **Read the box.** The shape and coating of the pan you use, will affect the temperature and cooking time. Do what the box tells you and remember to focus on signs of doneness, not time.

PRESENTATION

Again, the great thing about desserts is that they usually taste delicious no matter what they look like—but they're lots more enjoyable when they look as good as they taste. Because in **Half-Baked Gourmet: Desserts** so many recipes involve combining prepared ingredients, the presentation is particularly important. For puddings, a pretty wide-mouthed glass will make them especially beautiful. When you serve cookies, put just a few on a plate at a time; they will look more special that way.

FREEZER, FRIDGE, AND PANTRY

Following is a list of ingredients that you can keep on hand in order to make all the recipes in the book. All that's missing is the occasional fresh fruit.

IN THE FREEZER . . .

PASTRY
Phyllo (fillo) dough sheets
Pepperidge Farm® puff pastry
  sheets
Pepperidge Farm® puff pastry
  shells

PREPARED DESSERTS
Prepared pumpkin pie
Prepared cheesecake

ICE CREAM/SORBET
Chocolate ice cream
Chocolate sorbet
Vanilla ice cream
Strawberry sorbet
Mango sorbet
Coconut sorbet
Butter pecan ice cream
Chocolate chip cookie dough
  ice cream

FRUIT
Strawberries
Cherries
Rhubarb
Blueberries
Mixed berries
Sliced peaches
Mixed fruit
Birds Eye® raspberries in syrup

JUICE CONCENTRATES
Bacardi® Mixers–piña colada flavor
All-natural limeade concentrate
All-natural lemonade concentrate
Apple juice concentrate
Cranberry juice concentrate
Orange juice concentrate
Passion fruit juice concentrate

MISCELLANEOUS
Nondairy whipped topping

IN THE FRIDGE . . .

CRUSTS/DOUGHS
Pillsbury® classic pizza crust
Pillsbury® prepared pie crust
Pillsbury® crescent roll dough
Pillsbury® chocolate chip cookie
  dough
Pillsbury® gingerbread cookie
  dough
Pillsbury® sugar cookie dough
Pillsbury® ready-to-bake sugar
  cookies
Pillsbury® cinnamon rolls
Pillsbury® Golden Layers™
  buttermilk flaky biscuits

DAIRY
Eggnog
Vanilla yogurt
Chocolate pudding
Vanilla pudding
Cream cheese
Crumbled blue cheese
Mascarpone cheese

Sour cream
Half-and-half
Heavy cream
Milk
Eggs
Butter

IN THE PANTRY . . .

MIXES
Cookie
Betty Crocker® Bisquick all-
  purpose baking mix
Betty Crocker® oatmeal
  cookie mix
Betty Crocker® peanut butter
  cookie mix
Betty Crocker® sugar cookie mix

Cake
Duncan Hines® classic white
  cake mix
Duncan Hines® French vanilla
  cake mix
Duncan Hines® devil's food
  cake mix
Duncan Hines® angel food
  cake mix
Duncan Hines® classic golden
  cake mix
Duncan Hines® chewy fudge
  brownie mix
Duncan Hines® lemon cake mix
Dromedary® gingerbread cookie
  and cake mix
Dromedary® pound cake mix

Muffin

Jiffy® corn muffin mix
Pillsbury® date quick bread and
  muffin mix
Pillsbury® cranberry quick
  bread and muffin mix

CRUSTS

Graham cracker crust
Nabisco Oreo® cookie crust
Shortbread cookie crust
Mini phyllo dough shells

FILLINGS

Solo® pure almond paste
Libby's® easy pumpkin pie mix
Apple pie filling
Cherry pie filling
Blueberry pie filling

FROSTINGS

Vanilla frosting
Chocolate frosting
Cream cheese frosting

JAMS/JELLIES/SPREADS
(refrigerate after opening)

Strawberry pourable fruit
Seedless red raspberry jam
Seedless strawberry jam
Blueberry spreadable fruit
Raspberry spreadable fruit
Apple butter
Orange marmalade
Peach preserves
Grape jelly

Red currant jelly
Ginger preserves
Lemon curd
Chocolate hazelnut spread

TOPPINGS/SAUCES
(refrigerate after opening)

Magnolia® dulce de leche
Hershey's® hot fudge topping
Smucker's® caramel topping
Smucker's® walnuts in syrup
Rafetto® stem ginger in syrup
Marshmallow creme
Maple syrup
Honey

CHOCOLATE

Semisweet chocolate chips
Milk chocolate chips
Mini chocolate chips
White chocolate chunks
White chocolate

NUTS

Chopped pecans
Chopped hazelnuts
Whole hazelnuts
Pecan pieces
Pecan halves
Sliced almonds
Finely diced walnuts
Macadamia nuts
Sweetened flaked coconut
Honey-roasted peanuts
Planters® mixed nuts and
  raisins trail mix

CANDY

Farley's® starlight mints
Peppermint candy sticks
Hershey's® mini chocolate kisses
Caramels
Reese's® small peanut butter cups
Mini Snickers® bars
Mini York® peppermint patties
Andes® chocolate creme de
  menthe thins
Regular and mini marshmallows

COOKIES

Savoiardi biscuits (ladyfingers)
Nabisco Famous® chocolate
  wafers
Nabisco Oreo® chocolate
  sandwich cookies
Lazzaroni® Amaretti di Saronno
Nabisco® gingersnaps
Graham crackers
Regular and mini meringues

CAKES

Angel food cake
Entenmann's® all-butter loaf cake
Entenmann's® marble loaf cake

CEREALS

Chocolate-flavored crisp
  rice cereal
Granola
Kellogg's® corn flakes
Quaker® instant oatmeal–
  cinnamon and spice flavor

CANNED FRUIT

Sliced pears in light syrup
Canned pear halves in light and
  heavy syrup
Sliced peaches in heavy syrup
Del Monte® harvest spice sliced
  peaches
Apricot halves in heavy syrup
Dole® tropical fruit salad in
  passion fruit nectar
Mandarin orange segments
Whole purple plums in heavy
  syrup
Candied yams with brown sugar,
  cinnamon, and nutmeg
Pineapple rings

DRIED FRUIT

Candied orange peel
Del Monte® Pacific-style dried
  apricots
Candied cherries
Currants
Raisins
Harvest Bay® orchard fruit
  mixed dried fruit
Dried figs
Dried cranberries
Dried cherries

PUDDING MIXES

Cook-and-serve vanilla
  pudding mix
Cook-and-serve chocolate
  pudding mix
Nestlé® European-Style dark
  chocolate mousse mix

Cranberry gelatin dessert mix
Jell-O® instant flan mix
Goya® flan mix

DRINK MIXES

Chocolate milk mix
Hot cocoa mix
Chocolate-flavor syrup
Instant coffee powder
Medaglia D'Oro® instant
  espresso powder

JUICES
  (refrigerate after opening)

White grape juice
Cran-raspberry juice
Apricot nectar
Mango nectar
Guava nectar

BAKING GOODS

Cinnamon sugar
Pumpkin pie spice
Ground cinnamon
Cayenne pepper
Cream of tartar
Vanilla extract
Mint extract
Light corn syrup
Cornstarch
Unsweetened cocoa powder
Sugar
Confectioners' sugar
Light brown sugar
Flour
Cornstarch

WINE AND LIQUOR

Dry white wine
Sparkling wine
Sherry
Campari®
Grand Marnier
Dark rum
Coconut rum
Spiced rum
Amaretto
Coffee liqueur
Crème de cacao
Bourbon whiskey
Scotch whisky

MISCELLANEOUS

Knox® original unflavored
  gelatine
Coconut milk, regular and light
Cream of coconut
Sweetened condensed milk
Evaporated skim milk
Chestnut spread
Peanut butter
Almond syrup
Grenadine syrup
Balsamic vinegar
Ocean Spray® Cran-Fruit™
  cranberry-orange
  crushed fruit
Raisin cinnamon bread
Graham cracker crumbs
Peanut butter chips
Kraft Minute® quick-cooking
  tapioca
Kraft Minute® instant enriched
  long-grain white rice
Roland® instant polenta

The Cookie Jar... and Some Bars

Chocolate-Strawberry Thumbprints

If you have long fingernails, you might want to use the end of a teaspoon to make the indentations in the dough.

PREP TIME: 10 MINUTES • BAKE TIME: 10 MINUTES • MAKES: ABOUT 40 COOKIES

1 roll (18 ounces) refrigerated sugar cookie dough
1/2 cup seedless strawberry jam
1/3 cup chocolate chips

1. Heat oven to 350°F. Shape cookie dough into 1-inch balls and place them 2 inches apart on ungreased baking sheets. With your thumb, make an indentation in the center of each ball. Spoon rounded 1/4 teaspoon jam into each.

2. Bake until edges of cookies are golden, 10 to 12 minutes. Cool 1 minute on pan, then remove with a spatula to a wire rack to cool completely.

3. Place chocolate chips in a small sealable plastic bag, sealing the bag halfway. Microwave on medium-high for 45 seconds. Close the bag completely and massage it with your hands until chocolate is smooth. Cut a very small piece of one corner of the bag off with scissors or a sharp knife. Gently squeeze chocolate onto cookies in decorative patterns. Set aside until dry, about 1 hour.

VARIATION

Chocolate-Raspberry Thumbprints
Substitute seedless raspberry jam for the strawberry.

Inside-Out Chocolate Chip Cookies

Here, the chips are white and the cookie is dark, delicious chocolate.

PREP TIME: 10 MINUTES • BAKE TIME: 10 MINUTES • MAKES: ABOUT 40 COOKIES

1 package (1 pound 2.25 ounces)
   devil's food cake mix
1 1/2 sticks unsalted butter, melted
1 egg
1 1/3 cups white chocolate chunks

1. Heat oven to 350°F. In a medium bowl, combine cake mix, butter, and egg. Beat with an electric mixer on low speed 2 minutes, scraping down sides of bowl as necessary. Stir in white chocolate chunks.

2. Shape the dough into 1 1/2-inch balls and place them 2 inches apart on ungreased baking sheets.

3. Bake until cookies are set, about 10 minutes. Cool 1 minute on pan, then remove with a spatula to a wire rack to cool completely.

Maple-Pecan Drops

These perfect little nut drops are coated with a glossy maple glaze. For the best flavor, use pure maple syrup.

PREP TIME: 15 MINUTES • BAKE TIME: 10 MINUTES • MAKES: 48 COOKIES

1 roll (18 ounces) refrigerated sugar
    cookie dough
1 ½ cups pecans
2 cups confectioners' sugar
¾ cup maple syrup

1. Heat oven to 350°F. Grind pecans in food processor. Add cookie dough and pulse just until blended.

2. Shape the dough into 48 balls and place 2 inches apart on ungreased baking sheets. Bake until golden around edges, 10 to 13 minutes. Cool 1 minute on pan, then remove with a spatula to a wire rack to cool completely.

3. In a small bowl, combine the confectioners' sugar and the maple syrup and stir until completely blended. Dip tops of cookies in the mixture. Arrange cookies on a wire rack and set aside in a cool dry place until dry, 1 to 2 hours.

VARIATION

Chocolate-Pecan Drops
Omit the maple syrup and confectioners' sugar. Melt 1 cup semisweet chocolate chips. Dip cookies in the melted chocolate and let dry as directed above.

Peanut Butter and Jelly Sandwich Cookies

These fun cookies have all the great flavor of PB & J without the bread. The kids will love them!

PREP TIME: 25 MINUTES • BAKE TIME: 8 MINUTES • MAKES: ABOUT 50 SANDWICHES

1 package (1 pound 1.5 ounces)
    peanut butter cookie mix
1/3 cup vegetable oil
1/4 cup water
1 egg
2/3 cup grape jelly

1. Heat oven to 375°F. Stir together cookie mix, oil, water, and egg. Drop batter by level teaspoonfuls about 2 inches apart onto ungreased baking sheets.

2. Bake until edges of cookies are golden, 8 to 9 minutes. Cool 1 minute on pan, then remove with a spatula to a wire rack to cool completely.

3. Pair up the cookies so that sizes and shapes match. Spread 1/2 teaspoon of grape jelly on one of each pair of cookies and sandwich with the other.

Pecan Spirals

Making these cookies is easier than you might think. Just chill the dough for a few minutes if it gets too soft to work with.

PREP TIME: 20 MINUTES • COOK TIME: 7 MINUTES • CHILL TIME: 30 MINUTES
MAKES: ABOUT 48 COOKIES

1 cup (4 ounces) pecans
¼ cup firmly packed brown sugar
1 roll (18 ounces) refrigerated sugar
   cookie dough

1. In the bowl of a food processor, combine pecans and brown sugar. Pulse until finely ground.

2. Unwrap cookie dough, cut in half lengthwise, and place halves side by side between 2 pieces of wax paper. Using a rolling pin, roll dough to a 10 by 12-inch rectangle. Place dough on work surface with long side toward you. Remove top sheet of wax paper.

3. Spread surface evenly with nut mixture and roll up tightly into a 12-inch log, using the edge of the wax paper as a guide. Place the log on a small baking sheet and freeze until firm, about 30 minutes.

4. Heat oven to 350°F. Slice roll into ¼-inch slices. Place slices on baking sheets and bake until just golden, 7 to 11 minutes. Cool 1 minute on pan, then remove with a spatula to a wire rack to cool completely.

Lemon Cornmeal Cookies

These subtle and tender cookies are perfect for afternoon tea.

PREP TIME: 10 MINUTES • BAKE TIME: 14 MINUTES • MAKES: 24 COOKIES

1 package (8.5 ounces) corn muffin
   mix
¼ cup milk
1 egg
2 tablespoons butter, melted
2 tablespoons granulated sugar
2 teaspoons grated lemon zest
Confectioners' sugar, for dusting

1. Heat oven to 375°F. Prepare muffin mix according to package directions, using the milk and egg. Stir in butter, granulated sugar, and zest. Drop batter by rounded tablespoonfuls 2 inches apart onto a greased baking sheet.

2. Bake until edges are golden, 14 to 16 minutes. Cool 1 minute on pan, then remove with a spatula to a wire rack to cool completely. Dust with confectioners' sugar before serving.

Gingerbread Snowballs

These cute round cookies look like little snowballs. But inside they're chewy gingerbread. Surprise!

PREP TIME: 15 MINUTES • BAKE TIME: 11 MINUTES • MAKES: 48 COOKIES

1 roll (18 ounces) refrigerated
   gingerbread cookie dough
1 cup marshmallow creme dessert
   topping
1 $\frac{1}{3}$ cups sweetened flaked coconut

1. Heat oven to 350°F. Shape cookie dough into $\frac{3}{4}$-inch balls. Place 2 inches apart on ungreased baking sheets.

2. Bake until cookies are puffed and golden, 9 to 11 minutes. Cool 1 minute on pan, then remove with a spatula to a wire rack to cool completely.

3. Place marshmallow topping in a small bowl. Place flaked coconut in another bowl. Dip cookie tops in marshmallow, spinning them slightly, and then in coconut. Arrange cookies on a wax paper-lined baking sheet and set aside until no longer sticky.

Coconut-Walnut Cookies

These crisp little cookies will become favorites of nut lovers big and small.

PREP TIME: 10 MINUTES • BAKE TIME: 10 MINUTES • MAKES: 80 COOKIES

1 roll (18 ounces) refrigerated sugar
    cookie dough
1 cup chopped walnuts
¾ cup sweetened flaked coconut
2 tablespoons firmly packed light
    brown sugar

1. Heat oven to 350°F. Crumble cookie dough into a medium bowl. Add walnuts, coconut, and brown sugar and mix well with an electric mixer.

2. Shape the dough into ¾-inch balls and place them 2 inches apart on ungreased baking sheets.

3. Bake until golden brown, 10 to 13 minutes. Cool 1 minute on pan, then remove with a spatula to a wire rack to cool completely.

Gingerbread Stripers

These playful little cookies are a perfect addition to your Christmas cookie plate. If the dough gets too soft to move without it breaking, chill it between steps until it is just firm.

PREP TIME: 25 MINUTES • BAKE TIME: 10 MINUTES • CHILL TIME: 2 HOURS
MAKES: ABOUT 100 COOKIES

1 roll (18 ounces) refrigerated
   gingerbread cookie dough
1 roll (18 ounces) refrigerated
   sugar cookie dough

1. Unwrap gingerbread cookie dough, cut it in half lengthwise, and place the two halves side by side on a large sheet of wax paper. Cover with another piece of wax paper and roll with rolling pin into a 6 by 15-inch rectangle $\frac{1}{4}$ inch thick. Repeat with sugar cookie dough.

2. Chill both dough rectangles until firm. Remove the wax paper and place the sugar cookie dough on top of the gingerbread dough.

3. Cut the dough lengthwise into 4 even strips and stack them on top of each other so that colors alternate. Press together gently. Chill until firm.

4. Heat oven to 350°F. Cut the dough into 3 lengthwise strips and slice each strip crosswise into $\frac{1}{8}$-inch slices. Lay the slices on ungreased baking sheets and bake until set, about 10 minutes. Cool 1 minute on pan, then remove with a spatula to a wire rack to cool completely.

Cranberry-Ginger Oatmeal Cookies

These delicious chewy oatmeal cookies have extra ginger to satisfy grown-up tastes.

PREP TIME: 5 MINUTES • BAKE TIME: 12 MINUTES • MAKES: 24 COOKIES

1 package (1 pound 1.5 ounces)
    oatmeal cookie mix
1/3 cup vegetable oil
1 egg
3 tablespoons water
1/2 cup dried cranberries
1/4 cup white chocolate chips
3 tablespoons chopped crystallized
    ginger

1. Heat oven to 350°F. Prepare cookie mix according to package directions, using oil, egg, and water. Stir in cranberries, chocolate chips, and ginger. Drop batter by rounded tablespoonfuls 2 inches apart onto ungreased baking sheets.

2. Bake until edges are golden, 12 to 14 minutes. Cool 1 minute on pan, then remove with a spatula to a wire rack to cool complelely.

Double Orange Sugar Cookies

These would be ideal cookies to decorate like pumpkins for Halloween.

PREP TIME: 25 MINUTES • COOK TIME: 11 MINUTES • MAKES: ABOUT 5 1/2 DOZEN

1 package (1 pound 1.5 ounces) sugar
   cookie mix
1 stick (1/2 cup) butter, melted
1 egg
2/3 cup frozen orange juice
   concentrate, thawed
1 1/2 cups confectioners' sugar

1. Heat oven to 375°F. Combine cookie mix ingredients according to package directions, using the melted butter and egg and adding 6 tablespoons of the orange juice concentrate. Mix well.

2. Drop batter by heaping teaspoons 2 inches apart onto ungreased baking sheets.

3. Bake until edges are just golden, 11 to 13 minutes. Cool 1 minute on pan, then remove with a spatula to a wire rack to cool completely.

4. To make icing, combine confectioners' sugar and the remaining 4 tablespoons orange juice concentrate in a sealable plastic bag. Close the bag completely and massage it with your hands until blended. Cut a very small piece of one corner of the bag off with scissors or a sharp knife. Gently squeeze icing onto cookies in decorative patterns. Set aside until dry, about 1 hour.

Almond-Orange Crisps

Like lacy tuiles, these thin cookies can be shaped. While still warm, wrap them around a rolling pin or large dowel to curl. Remove and then cool completely.

PREP TIME: 10 MINUTES • COOK TIME: 10 MINUTES • MAKES: ABOUT 56 COOKIES

1 package (1 pound 1.5 ounces) sugar
    cookie mix
²/₃ cup orange marmalade
1 stick (½ cup) butter, melted
1 cup sliced almonds

1. Heat oven to 350°F. In a large bowl, combine sugar cookie mix, marmalade, and butter. Stir until well blended. Add almonds and mix well. Drop batter by rounded teaspoons 2 inches apart onto ungreased baking sheets.

2. Bake 10 minutes until light golden. Let cool 1 minute on pan. Shape if desired, then place on a wire rack to cool completely.

Candy Pizza

This big cookie will bring a smile to everyone's lips, even before they take a bite.

PREP TIME: 12 MINUTES • COOK TIME: 18 MINUTES • MAKES: 8 LARGE WEDGES

1 roll (18 ounces) refrigerated sugar
    cookie dough
$1/2$ cup milk chocolate chips
$1/2$ cup semisweet chocolate chips
$1/2$ cup white chocolate chips
$1/2$ cup chopped pecans

1. Heat oven to 350°F. Unwrap dough and, using floured hands, press it evenly onto a greased 14-inch pizza pan.

2. Sprinkle chocolate chips and nuts evenly over the dough.

3. Bake until edges are light brown and center is puffed, 18 to 20 minutes. Cool in pan on a wire rack and cut into wedges.

VARIATION

Krazy Kids Kandy Pizza
Substitute $1/2$ cup M&M's® for the white chocolate chips and $1/2$ cup gummy bears for the nuts.

Puffy Chocolate Marshmallow Sandwiches

These seconds-to-make sandwich cookies are a perfect last-minute treat for the kids . . . or you.

PREP TIME: 1 MINUTE • COOK TIME: 45 SECONDS • MAKES: 8 SANDWICHES

16 chocolate wafer cookies
8 marshmallows

1. Place 8 of the cookies upside down on a nonmetal plate. Top each cookie with 1 marshmallow, flat-side down.

2. Microwave on medium-high power until marshmallows puff up several inches, about 45 seconds.

3. Remove plate from microwave and top each marshmallow with another chocolate cookie. Press down gently until the marshmallow puffs just past the cookie edges. Cool to room temperature, about 1 minute, and serve.

Mocha Swirl Brownies

These easy-to-make brownies satisfy both chocolate lovers and coffee lovers with one great bar.

PREP TIME: 20 MINUTES • BAKE TIME: 35 MINUTES • MAKES: 24 BARS

1 package (21 ounces) chewy fudge
    brownie mix
1/2 cup vegetable oil
1/4 cup water
4 large eggs
1 package (8 ounces) cream cheese,
    softened
1/2 cup sugar
1 tablespoon flour
2 teaspoons instant coffee granules

1. Heat oven to 350°F. In a large bowl, stir together the brownie mix, vegetable oil, water, and 3 of the eggs until well blended. Spread two-thirds of the batter evenly in a foil-lined and lightly greased 13 x 9-inch baking pan.

2. In a second large bowl, beat cream cheese, sugar, flour, coffee granules, and the remaining egg with an electric mixer on medium speed until blended. Spread gently over brownie layer. Dot with remaining fudge batter and swirl by making circles with a toothpick.

3. Bake until a toothpick inserted 1 inch from edge comes out clean, about 35 minutes. Cool completely in pan on a wire rack. Remove foil, and using a sharp knife, cut into bars.

VARIATION

Amaretto Swirl Brownies
Substitute 1 teaspoon almond extract for the instant coffee granules.

Rocky Road Brownies

These sweet treats will become a family favorite after the first bite. Don't look for the marshmallows—they bake right in.

PREP TIME: 10 MINUTES • BAKE TIME: 34 MINUTES • MAKES: 16 BROWNIES

1 package (21 ounces) chewy fudge
    brownie mix
1/2 cup vegetable oil
1/4 cup water
2 large eggs
1 1/2 cups chopped walnuts
2 cups mini marshmallows

1. Heat oven to 350°F. In a large bowl, stir together brownie mix, vegetable oil, water, and eggs until well blended. Stir in walnuts and marshmallows. Spread batter evenly in a foil-lined and lightly greased 9-inch-square baking pan.

2. Bake until a toothpick inserted 2 inches from the center comes out clean, 34 to 37 minutes. Cool completely in pan on a wire rack. Remove foil, and using a sharp knife, cut into squares.

Crème de Cacao Brownie Bites

These fudgy bites have a little something extra that makes them adult-only treats.

PREP TIME: 15 MINUTES • BAKE TIME: 37 MINUTES • MAKES: 36 BROWNIES

1 package (21 ounces) chewy fudge
    brownie mix
$1/2$ cup vegetable oil
$1 1/4$ cups crème de cacao
2 large eggs
$1 1/4$ cups confectioners' sugar

1. Heat oven to 350°F. In a large bowl, stir together the brownie mix, vegetable oil, 1 cup of the crème de cacao, and eggs until well blended. Spread batter evenly in a foil-lined and lightly greased 9-inch-square baking pan.

2. Bake until a toothpick inserted 2 inches from center comes out clean, 34 to 37 minutes.

3. Mix confectioners' sugar with the remaining $1/4$ cup crème de cacao. Spread over warm brownies. Cool in pan on a wire rack until topping is firm, at least 4 hours. Remove foil, and using a sharp knife, cut into squares.

VARIATION

Crème de Menthe Brownie Bites
Substitute crème de menthe for the crème de cacao.

Nut 'n' Honey Bars

These nut-covered bars are sophisticated and delicious.

PREP TIME: 10 MINUTES • BAKE/COOK TIME: 33 MINUTES • MAKES: 24 BARS

1 roll (18 ounces) refrigerated sugar
   cookie dough
¾ cup firmly packed brown sugar
½ cup honey
½ cup heavy cream
¾ cup chopped pecans
¾ cup chopped walnuts
¾ cup sliced almonds

1. Heat oven to 350°F. Crumble cookie dough into an ungreased 13 x 9-inch baking pan. Press it evenly with your fingers to form a crust. Bake 15 minutes.

2. In a small saucepan, combine sugar, honey, and cream. Heat to boiling over medium heat and cook 3 minutes. Stir in all the nuts and spread over crust.

3. Bake until set, 15 to 17 minutes. Cool completely in pan on a wire rack. Using a sharp knife, cut into bars.

Raspberry Linzer Bars

These fantastic bars have all the flavors of a classic Linzer tart, but they are so much easier to make.

PREP TIME: 20 MINUTES • BAKE TIME: 40 MINUTES • MAKES: 18 BARS

1 package (1 pound 1.5 ounces) sugar
   cookie mix
1/2 cup almond paste
5 tablespoons unsalted butter
1/2 teaspoon ground cinnamon
1 egg
1/2 cup seedless raspberry jam

1. Heat oven to 375°F. In the bowl of a food processor, combine sugar cookie mix, almond paste, butter, and cinnamon. Pulse until mixture makes fine crumbs. Add egg and pulse until blended.

2. Press two-thirds of the dough into the bottom of a foil-lined and lightly greased 9-inch-square baking pan. Spread jam over the dough. Crumble remaining dough over the jam.

3. Bake until golden, about 40 minutes. Cool completely in pan on a wire rack. Remove foil, and using a sharp knife, cut into bars.

Lovely Lemon Bars

These are the quickest, easiest lemon bars you could ever dream of making.

PREP TIME: 10 MINUTES • BAKE TIME: 35 MINUTES • MAKES: 24 SQUARES

1 roll (18 ounces) refrigerated sugar
    cookie dough
1 jar (11 ounces) lemon curd
¼ cup confectioners' sugar

1. Heat oven to 350°F. Crumble sugar cookie dough into the bottom of a foil-lined 13 x 9-inch pan. Press it evenly with your fingers to form a crust. Bake until light golden brown, 11 to 13 minutes.

2. Spread the hot crust evenly with lemon curd and bake until bubbly on the edges, 20 minutes longer.

3. Cool in pan on a wire rack 30 minutes, then dust with confectioners' sugar. Let cool completely. Remove foil, and using a sharp knife, cut into squares.

Oatmeal Figgy Squares

These super squares are like little oatmeal fig sandwiches.

PREP TIME: 25 MINUTES • COOK TIME: 40 MINUTES • MAKES: 25 SQUARES

1 navel orange
1 1/2 cups chopped dried figs
1/2 cup plus 3 tablespoons water
1 package (1 pound 1.5 ounces)
    oatmeal cookie mix
1/3 cup vegetable oil
1 egg

1. Heat oven to 350°F. Grate the zest of the orange and squeeze its juice into a small saucepan. Add figs and 1/2 cup water. Heat mixture to boiling. Adjust heat and simmer until figs are softened, about 10 minutes, stirring occasionally. Transfer mixture to the bowl of a food processor and purée until smooth.

2. Prepare oatmeal cookie dough according to package directions, using the vegetable oil, egg, and remaining 3 tablespoons water. Press half the dough into a foil-lined 9-inch-square baking pan. Spread evenly with fig mixture. Top with remaining dough and press down gently.

3. Bake until puffed and golden, about 30 minutes. Cool completely in pan on a wire rack. Remove foil, and using a sharp knife, cut into squares.

Coconut Spice Bars

These tasty cookies will be a welcome addition to any holiday cookie plate.

PREP TIME: 10 MINUTES • BAKE TIME: 35 MINUTES • MAKES: 24 SERVINGS

1 package (1 pound 1.5 ounces) sugar
    cookie mix
1 stick (½ cup) butter, melted
5 large eggs
2 teaspoons pumpkin pie spice
1 package (10 ounces) sweetened
    flaked coconut

1. Heat oven to 350°F. In a large bowl, stir together sugar cookie mix, melted butter, one of the eggs, and the pumpkin pie spice until well blended.

2. Spread mixture into a foil-lined and lightly greased 13 x 9-inch baking pan. Bake 15 minutes. Remove pan from oven and sprinkle top of crust evenly with coconut. In a medium bowl, lightly beat the remaining 4 eggs and drizzle them evenly over the coconut.

3. Return pan to the oven and bake 20 minutes longer. Cool completely in pan on a wire rack. Remove foil, and using a sharp knife, cut into bars.

Blueberry Cheesecake Bars

These simple bars are perfect when you want just a bite of cheesecake.

PREP TIME: 15 MINUTES • BAKE TIME: 35 MINUTES • MAKES: 24 BARS

1 roll (18 ounces) refrigerated sugar
    cookie dough
12 ounces cream cheese, softened
2 eggs
$\frac{1}{3}$ cup sugar
2 teaspoons grated lemon zest
1$\frac{1}{2}$ cups blueberry pie filling

1. Heat oven to 350°F. Break up dough and press it evenly into the bottom of a foil-lined and lightly greased 13 x 9-inch baking pan.

2. In a medium-sized bowl, beat cream cheese, eggs, sugar, and lemon zest with an electric mixer until smooth and thick. Spread cheese mixture over cookie dough. Dollop blueberry pie filling on cheese; swirl with a knife or small metal spatula.

3. Bake 40 minutes. Cool to room temperature, then refrigerate in pan until chilled. Using a sharp knife, cut into bars.

Caramel Granola Bars

These great granola bars are so much better than store-bought ones.

20 caramels
2 tablespoons water
3 cups granola

1. Heat oven to 300°F. Combine caramels and water in a medium non-metal bowl. Microwave on high until almost completely melted, 2 to 3 minutes, stirring every 30 seconds. Continue stirring until completely smooth.

2. Crumble granola into the melted caramel and mix until combined. Press mixture into a foil-lined and lightly greased 9-inch-square baking pan.

3. Bake 20 minutes (the bars will still be very soft). Cool in pan 20 minutes, and using a sharp knife, cut into bars. Let cool completely until firm and remove foil.

Coconut Snow Haystacks

These are elegant enough for a fancy afternoon tea, but easy enough to make any day.

PREP TIME: 5 MINUTES • CHILL TIME: 30 MINUTES • COOK TIME: 15 MINUTES

MAKES: 20 STACKS

1 $^3/_4$ **cups sweetened flaked coconut**

8 ounces white chocolate chips

1. Heat oven to 350°F. Spread the coconut in a square metal baking pan and toast until partially golden, about 15 minutes, stirring it twice during cooking.

2. Place white chocolate chips in a medium nonmetal bowl and microwave on medium-high power until melted, about 2 minutes.

3. Stir coconut into the melted chocolate. Using a tablespoon of coconut mixture each, make 1 $^1/_2$-inch-high stacks on a parchment- or foil-lined baking sheet. Refrigerate until firm, about 30 minutes.

VARIATION

Dark Chocolate Haystacks

Substitute semisweet chocolate chips for the white chocolate.

Milk Chocolate Haystacks

Substitute milk chocolate chips for the white chocolate.

Coconut Cereal Snacks

These glistening little balls are surprisingly delicate. Be sure to let the mixture cool slightly before shaping so that you don't burn your fingers.

PREP TIME: 25 MINUTES • COOK TIME: 5 MINUTES • MAKES: ABOUT 2 DOZEN BALLS

½ stick (¼ cup) butter
1 package (10 ounces) large
    marshmallows
6 cups sweetened corn flakes cereal
¾ cup flaked coconut

1. In a medium saucepan over low heat, melt butter. Add marshmallows, and cook until they are melted, stirring constantly. Remove from heat.

2. Add cereal and coconut immediately, and mix gently until evenly coated. Let cool 1 minute.

3. Using lightly greased fingertips, form loose, 2-inch balls with the warm mixture, and drop them onto a wax paper–lined baking sheet. Cool completely, about 15 minutes.

Triple Chocolate Crispy Treats

These chocolate, chocolate, and more chocolate treats will wow your family every time.

PREP TIME: 10 MINUTES • COOK TIME: 8 MINUTES • MAKES: 24 SQUARES

$1/2$ stick ($1/4$ cup) butter

1 package (10 ounces) marshmallows

2 tablespoons cocoa powder

6 cups chocolate-flavored crisp rice cereal

$1/2$ cup mini chocolate chips

1. In a large nonstick saucepan over low heat, melt butter. Add marshmallows and cocoa powder. Stir until marshmallows are melted. Remove from heat. Stir in cereal until completely blended. Stir in mini chocolate chips.

2. Spray a 13 x 9-inch baking pan with nonstick cooking spray. Spread mixture in pan, pressing down firmly with greased fingertips. Cool completely in pan. With a sharp knife, cut into squares.

VARIATION

Chocolate-Peanut Butter Crispy Treats
Substitute $1/2$ cup peanut butter chips for the mini chocolate chips.

Nutty Meringue Chews

These nutty little squares are perfect treats when you want just a bite of sweetness.

PREP TIME: 5 MINUTES • COOK TIME: 5 MINUTES • MAKES: 36 CHEWS

½ stick (¼ cup) butter
1 bag (10 ounces) marshmallows
4 cups chopped pecans
½ teaspoon ground cinnamon

1. Line an 8-inch-square baking pan with foil and grease lightly. Line the bottom with wax paper.

2. In a medium saucepan over medium heat, melt the butter. Add marshmallows and stir until melted. Remove from heat and mix in the pecans and cinnamon.

3. Press the mixture into prepared pan. Refrigerate until firm. Remove foil and wax paper, and, using a sharp knife, cut into squares.

Fruit and Nut Chocolate Tartlets

These little chocolate candies are a sweet addition to the dessert tray.

PREP TIME: 5 MINUTES • **CHILL TIME: 1 HOUR** • **MAKES: 12 TARTLETS**

1½ cups chocolate chips
1 package (6 ounces) mixed nuts and
    raisins trail mix

1. Place chocolate chips in a small nonmetal bowl. Microwave on medium-high power until partially melted. Stir until completely melted. Stir in trail mix.

2. Spoon the chocolate mixture into 12 paper-lined muffin cups, dividing evenly.

3. Cool to room temperature and refrigerate until solid, about 1 hour.

Chocolate-Peanut Butter Cookie Cups

A chocolate-peanut butter cup baked into a devil's food cookie cup—that's three great tastes that taste great together.

PREP TIME: 12 MINUTES • BAKE TIME: 8 MINUTES • MAKES: 24 COOKIES

1 package (1 pound 2.25 ounces)
   devil's food cake mix
1 1/2 sticks (3/4 cup) unsalted butter,
   melted
1 egg
24 small peanut butter cups,
   unwrapped

1. Heat oven to 350°F. In a medium bowl, combine cake mix, butter, and egg. Beat with an electric mixer on low speed 2 minutes, scraping down sides of bowl as necessary. Refrigerate mixture until firm, about 30 minutes.

2. Roll cookie dough into twenty-four 1-inch balls. Place each ball in a small (1 3/4-inch) paper baking cup and place cups 1 inch apart on a baking sheet. Press a peanut butter cup halfway into each dough ball.

3. Bake until the cookies are puffed and set, 8 to 12 minutes. Cool completely in baking cups on wire rack.

Snickermuffin Surprises

A tiny Snickers® candy bar is hidden inside each cookie cupcake. Surprise!

PREP TIME: 10 MINUTES • COOK TIME: 14 MINUTES • MAKES: 20 COOKIES

20 miniature Snickers® bars (9 grams each)
1 package (18 ounces) ready-to-bake sugar cookies

1. Heat oven to 350°F. Unwrap candy bars. Place one candy in the center of each cookie dough round. Wrap the dough around the candy and roll between hands to enclose candy in center. Repeat with remaining candies and dough.

2. Place each dough ball in a small (1¾-inch) paper baking cup and place cups 1 inch apart on a baking sheet.

3. Bake until puffed and just golden, 14 to 16 minutes. Cool completely in baking cups on wire rack.

Mint Candy Melts

Mint candy lovers now have a cookie to enjoy, too.

PREP TIME: 5 MINUTES • COOK TIME: 14 MINUTES • MAKES: 20 COOKIES

1 package (18 ounces) ready-to-bake
    sugar cookies
20 mini chocolate-covered peppermint
    candies (12 grams each)

1. Heat oven to 350°F. Place cookie dough rounds 2 inches apart on ungreased baking sheets. Unwrap candies and place one candy on top of each round.

2. Bake until just golden on edges, 14 to 16 minutes. Cool 2 minutes on cookie sheet and then transfer to a wire rack to cool completely.

Chocolate-Hazelnut Kisses

These elegant-looking cookies are ideal for a fancy party.

PREP TIME: 15 MINUTES • COOK TIME: 2 MINUTES • MAKES: ABOUT 65 COOKIES

¾ cup semisweet chocolate chips

1 cup chopped hazelnuts

1 package (5.1 ounces) mini meringue
    kisses

1. Place chocolate chips in a nonmetal bowl and microwave on high until almost melted, about 2 minutes. Stir until completely melted.

2. Place hazelnuts in a small shallow bowl. Dip each meringue kiss sideways into chocolate to coat one side. Gently scrape off excess chocolate, then dip in chopped nuts. Arrange cookies on a wax paper-lined baking sheet and set aside in a cool dry place until dry, about 2 hours.

On, In, Or Under a Crust

Cranberry-Walnut Tart

This perfect autumn tart is just right when you want something that's not too rich.

PREP TIME: 10 MINUTES • COOK TIME: 50 MINUTES • MAKES: 12 SERVINGS

1 refrigerated pie crust (from a
   15-ounce package)

3 eggs

²/₃ cup light corn syrup

²/₃ cup firmly packed light brown sugar

½ stick (¼ cup) butter, melted and
   cooled

1 teaspoon vanilla extract

1⅓ cups chopped walnuts

1 container (12 ounces) cranberry-
   orange crushed fruit

1. Heat oven to 425°F. Fit pie crust into a 10- to 11-inch tart pan with removable bottom.

2. Whisk together the eggs, corn syrup, brown sugar, butter, and vanilla. Stir in the walnuts and crushed fruit. Pour filling into crust.

3. Bake 20 minutes, then reduce heat to 350°F. Continue baking until filling is puffed and golden, 30 to 40 minutes longer. Cool in pan on wire rack to room temperature before serving.

Easiest Strawberry Tart

Be sure not to break up the berries or the filling will get very runny and won't stay in the crust. A little leak is fine, though.

PREP TIME: 10 MINUTES • BAKE TIME: 25 MINUTES • MAKES: 10 SERVINGS

1 refrigerated pie crust (from a
    15-ounce package)
3 cups frozen strawberries, thawed
    and quartered
1/3 cup sugar
2 tablespoons cornstarch

1. Heat oven to 425°F. Place pie crust on a foil-lined baking sheet. In a large bowl, very gently toss berries with sugar and cornstarch. Pile berries in the center of the crust, leaving a 2-inch border.

2. Fold up the edges of the crust to partially cover the fruit, pinching them together.

3. Bake until golden and bubbly, 25 to 30 minutes. Cool on pan at least 10 minutes before removing.

VARIATION

Easiest Cherry Tart
Substitute halved frozen cherries for the strawberries.

Pear-Berry Custard Tart

This lovely, simple tart has classic French flavors.

PREP TIME: 15 MINUTES • COOK TIME: 1 HOUR 15 MINUTES • MAKES: 8 SERVINGS

1 sheet frozen puff pastry (from a
   17.3-ounce package), thawed
1 can (16 ounces) pear halves in light
   syrup, drained and thinly sliced
3 eggs
½ cup sugar
1½ cups heavy cream
½ teaspoon grated lemon zest
1 cup frozen raspberries, thawed

1. Heat oven to 350°F. Unfold the sheet of puff pastry onto a lightly floured board. Roll to a 13-inch square. Fit the pastry into a 10-inch tart pan with removable bottom, allowing the pastry to overlap the rim. Place a piece of foil over pastry and weigh down with raw rice or dried beans.

2. Bake until light brown, about 25 minutes. Remove aluminum foil and weights from shell. Bake 5 minutes longer. Remove from oven and allow pastry to cool for 5 to 10 minutes.

3. Reduce oven temperature to 325°F. Place tart pan on a baking sheet. Arrange pear slices over the bottom of the tart. In a medium bowl, whisk together the eggs, sugar, cream, and lemon zest. Pour mixture over the sliced pears. Scatter raspberries over surface. Bake for 45 minutes or until just set.

4. Remove from oven and break off outer edges of crust, if desired. Serve warm or at room temperature.

Death-by-Chocolate Tart

Creamy chocolate on crisp chocolate makes this tart a chocoholic's fantasy.

PREP TIME: 20 MINUTES • COOK TIME: 22 MINUTES • CHILL TIME: 2 HOURS
MAKES: 12 SERVINGS

1 roll (18 ounces) refrigerated sugar
   cookie dough
3 tablespoons unsweetened cocoa
   powder
2 cups chocolate chips
1/2 cup heavy cream
3/4 cup hot fudge sauce

1. Heat oven to 350°F. Crumble cookie dough into the bowl of a food processor. Add cocoa powder and pulse just until blended.

2. Press cookie dough mixture into the bottom and up the sides of an ungreased 10- to 11-inch tart pan with a removable bottom. Bake for 20 to 22 minutes or until puffed and golden. When cool enough to touch, press down the center of the cookie to form a tart shell. Cool completely, about 30 minutes.

3. Place chocolate chips in a medium bowl. In a small saucepan, heat cream until almost boiling. Pour over chips. Stir until smooth and blended. Stir in fudge sauce. Pour filling into tart shell and refrigerate until set. Serve chilled.

Lemon Mascarpone Tart

This great grown-up tart is so simple to make.

PREP TIME: 15 MINUTES • COOK TIME: 12 MINUTES • CHILL TIME: 1 HOUR

MAKES: 12 SERVINGS

1 refrigerated pie crust (from a
   15-ounce package)
1 jar (11 ounces) lemon curd
1 cup mascarpone cheese, softened
1 container (8 ounces) sour cream
1/3 cup sugar

1. Heat oven to 425°F. Fit crust into a 9-inch tart pan with removable bottom. Bake until golden, 12 minutes. Cool to room temperature.

2. Spread lemon curd in tart shell. In a medium bowl, stir together the mascarpone, sour cream, and sugar. Spoon in dollops over the curd and gently spread to cover the curd. Refrigerate and serve chilled.

Pineapple-Coconut Tart

Piña coladas don't have to come in a glass. This simple tart is a beautiful way to end a simple meal.

PREP TIME: 10 MINUTES • COOK TIME: 35 MINUTES • MAKES: 8 SERVINGS

1 sheet frozen puff pastry (from a
    17.3-ounce package), thawed
¼ cup cream of coconut
7 pineapple rings (from a 20-ounce
    can)
⅓ cup sweetened flaked coconut

1. Heat oven to 375°F. Fit pastry sheet into a 10-inch tart pan with removable bottom. Spread with cream of coconut. Arrange pineapple rings over to just fit in pan and sprinkle with flaked coconut.

2. Bake until pastry is puffed and golden, 35 to 40 minutes. Cool in pan on wire rack to room temperature before serving.

Banana-Macadamia Tart Tatin

The easiest way to cut the right-sized circle from the puff pastry is to invert a pan over it and trace its outline.

PREP TIME: 5 MINUTES • BAKE/COOK TIME: 18 MINUTES • MAKES: 6 SERVINGS

1 sheet frozen puff pastry (from a
    17.3-ounce package), thawed
4 large bananas
1 tablespoon butter
$1/2$ cup finely chopped macadamias
$1/4$ cup caramel sauce

1. Heat oven to 375°F. Roll pastry sheet to an 11-inch square. Cut an 11-inch round from the puff pastry. Peel bananas and cut them in half lengthwise.

2. In a 10-inch ovenproof skillet over medium heat, melt butter. Arrange bananas in pan in concentric circles, rounded-side down. Cook over medium-high heat until bananas begin to brown, about 3 minutes. Sprinkle with nuts and drizzle with caramel sauce. Cook 2 minutes longer.

3. Top bananas with pastry round. Place in oven and bake until crust is golden, 13 to 15 minutes. Let cool 10 minutes. Invert onto serving plate and serve immediately.

Thin Apple Tarts

These elegant tarts are a not-too-sweet dessert for grown-ups. Keep the kids away and save them for yourself.

PREP TIME: 8 MINUTES   •   COOK TIME: 30 MINUTES   •   MAKES: 4 SERVINGS

1 sheet frozen puff pastry (from a
   17.3-ounce package), thawed
¼ cup apple butter
1 Granny Smith apple, peeled, cored,
   and very thinly sliced
1 tablespoon butter, cut in small bits
4 teaspoons sugar

1. Heat oven to 400°F. Roll puff pastry into a 10-inch square. Cut it in half to make 2 rectangles. Brush the edges of the dough with water and fold them over ¼ inch all around. Place dough strips on a baking sheet.

2. Spread the inner rectangle of each with apple butter, then overlap the apple slices on top. Dot with butter, then sprinkle with sugar.

3. Bake until crust is puffed and golden, about 30 minutes. Let cool slightly. Cut each tart crosswise into 2 pieces. Serve warm or at room temperature.

Chocolate Chip Cookie Ice Cream Tart

Chocolate chips on chocolate chips on chocolate chips . . .

PREP TIME: 12 MINUTES • COOK TIME: 16 MINUTES • FREEZE TIME: 2 HOURS

MAKES: 16 SERVINGS

1 roll (18 ounces) refrigerated
    chocolate chip cookie dough
1 quart chocolate chip cookie dough
    ice cream, slightly softened
1/3 cup mini chocolate chips

1. Heat oven to 350°F. Press dough into bottom of ungreased 10- or 11-inch springform pan. Bake until golden, 16 to 18 minutes. Cool completely. Do not remove the cookie from pan.

2. Spread the cookie with ice cream and sprinkle with chocolate chips. Freeze until firm, 2 to 3 hours. Remove sides from pan to serve.

Lemon Meringue Tartlets

These perfect little tartlets take seconds to make and are elegant enough to serve at a fancy dinner party.

PREP TIME: 1 MINUTE • COOK TIME: 30 SECONDS • MAKES: 15 SERVINGS

1 package (2.1 ounces) mini phyllo
    dough shells
²/₃ cup lemon curd
²/₃ cup marshmallow topping

1. Heat broiler. Place oven rack 8 inches from heat.

2. Arrange dough shells on a baking sheet. Spoon 2 teaspoons of lemon curd into each. Top each with 2 teaspoons marshmallow topping.

3. Broil tartlets until just golden, about 30 seconds. Cool to room temperature and serve.

VARIATION

Chocolate Meringue Tartlets
Replace lemon curd with prepared chocolate pudding. (Do not use instant pudding.)

Cranberry-Lemon Tartlets

You can freeze fresh cranberries in sealable plastic bags for months. They defrost quickly and taste perfect.

PREP TIME: 10 MINUTES • COOK TIME: 20 MINUTES • MAKES: 4 SERVINGS

1⅓ cups graham cracker crumbs
½ stick (¼ cup) butter, melted
1 package (8 ounces) cream cheese, softened
⅓ cup lemon curd
2 large eggs
7 tablespoons sugar
2 tablespoons red currant jelly
1 cup cranberries

1. Heat oven to 350°F. In a small bowl, combine graham cracker crumbs and butter. Blend together with fingers and pat into the bottom and up the sides of four 4¾-inch tartlet pans with removable bottoms. Place pans on baking sheets.

2. In a medium bowl, combine cream cheese, lemon curd, eggs, and 4 tablespoons of the sugar. Beat until smooth with an electric mixer. Spoon into tart shells and bake until puffed and just beginning to brown on edges, about 20 minutes. Cool on wire racks and chill until ready to serve.

3. In a small saucepan, combine jelly, the remaining 3 tablespoons of sugar, and 1 tablespoon water. Heat over medium heat until sugar is dissolved. Add cranberries and cook just until berries pop. Cool slightly. Remove tartlets from pans and place on serving plates. Spoon cranberry mixture in the center of each tartlet, dividing evenly. Serve immediately.

Brown Sugar-Pear Galettes

Make these beautiful tarts in the autumn when pears are in season and at their peak.

PREP TIME: 15 MINUTES • **COOK TIME: 25 MINUTES** • **MAKES: 6 SERVINGS**

1 package (10 ounces) frozen puff
   pastry shells, thawed
3 ripe Bartlett pears, peeled, cored,
   and sliced
²⁄₃ cup firmly packed light brown sugar
1 teaspoon ground cinnamon
2 tablespoons butter

1. Heat oven to 400°F. Roll out pastry shells into 5-inch rounds and place them on a foil-lined baking sheet. Arrange pear slices over the center of each round.

2. Sprinkle pear slices with about 2 tablespoons of the brown sugar and ¹⁄₈ teaspoon of the cinnamon. Dot each with 1 teaspoon of the butter.

3. Bake until golden, about 25 minutes, basting pears occasionally with juices from the pan. Serve warm or at room temperature.

Plum Crostata

The secret to making this tart is sealing the edges without letting any liquid spill out. Work quickly and be sure to seal everything up completely.

PREP TIME: 10 MINUTES • COOK TIME: 35 MINUTES • MAKES: 6 TO 8 SERVINGS

1 can (30 ounces) whole purple plums in heavy syrup, drained well
2½ teaspoons cornstarch
2 tablespoons raspberry spreadable fruit
1 sheet frozen puff pastry (from a 17.3-ounce package), thawed
1 egg, mixed with 1 tablespoon water
1 teaspoon sugar

1. Heat oven to 400°F. Tear each plum into halves and remove pits. In a medium bowl, toss plums with cornstarch, then gently mix in spreadable fruit. Roll out pastry on a lightly floured surface to an 11-inch square.

2. Place pastry on a baking sheet. Spoon plums over center of the crust, leaving a 2-inch border. Fold pastry over the fruit, folding and overlapping the edges but leaving some of the fruit exposed in the center. Brush crust with egg mixture and sprinkle with sugar.

3. Bake on bottom oven rack until pastry is golden and filling is bubbly, about 35 to 40 minutes. Serve warm or at room temperature.

Pear-Cranberry Pie

This might just be the easiest fruit pie ever. If you can't find sliced pears, use pear halves and slice them.

PREP TIME: 8 MINUTES • COOK TIME: 1 HOUR 15 MINUTES • MAKES: 8 TO 10 SERVINGS

2 refrigerated pastry crusts (from a 15-ounce package)

3 cans (15 ounces each) sliced pears in light syrup, drained

1 container (12 ounces) cranberry-orange crushed fruit

$\frac{1}{3}$ cup sugar

3 tablespoons cornstarch

$\frac{1}{4}$ teaspoon ground cinnamon

1 tablespoon butter, cut in small pieces

1. Heat oven to 425°F. Line a 9-inch glass pie plate with one of the crusts. In a medium bowl, combine pears, crushed fruit, sugar, cornstarch, and cinnamon. Mix gently but thoroughly. Spread pear mixture in pie shell. Dot with butter.

2. Cut remaining crust into 1-inch strips. Weave the strips in a loose basket weave on the top of the pie. Secure the edges by sealing with water, pinching together, and folding under excess crust.

3. Bake 15 minutes, then reduce heat to 375°F and continue baking until filling is bubbly, about 1 hour. Cool in pan on wire rack to room temperature before serving.

Cranberry-Raspberry Pie

Serve this pretty pie with freshly whipped cream for a beautiful presentation.

PREP TIME: 10 MINUTES • **COOK TIME: 5 MINUTES** • **MAKES: 8 SERVINGS**

1 graham cracker crust (6 ounces)

1 egg white

1 package (3 ounces) cranberry
   gelatin dessert

1 1/2 cups cran-raspberry juice

1 package (12 ounces) frozen
   raspberries

Whipped cream, for serving

1. Brush the crust with egg white and bake according to directions for "golden crust." Let cool to room temperature. Prepare cranberry gelatin, substituting cran-raspberry juice for the water and reducing the cold liquid to 1/2 cup. Add the berries to the warm liquid and stir gently. Refrigerate until mixture is just beginning to jell, about half an hour.

2. Stir berries into cranberry-raspberry mixture. Pour into crust and refrigerate until set. Serve with whipped cream.

Pecan Toffee Pumpkin Pie

Go ahead and cheat—tell everyone this dessert is homemade. I won't tell if you don't.

PREP TIME: 5 MINUTES • COOK TIME: 1 HOUR 10 MINUTES • MAKES: 8 SERVINGS

1 frozen pumpkin pie (37 ounces)
½ stick (¼ cup) butter, softened
¾ cup firmly packed light brown sugar
¾ cup pecans, chopped

1. Heat oven to 375°F. Bake frozen pumpkin pie until edges are set but center of pie is slightly wet, about 55 minutes.

2. Increase oven heat to 400°F. In a medium bowl, using a rubber spatula, cream together butter and brown sugar. Fold in pecans. Gently sprinkle onto hot pumpkin pie to cover and bake until topping is just browned, 10 to 15 minutes. Cool in pan on wire rack to room temperature before serving.

Caramel-Apple Pie

Two favorites have finally made it under one crust.

PREP TIME: 20 MINUTES • COOK TIME: 1 HOUR 10 MINUTES • MAKES: 8 SERVINGS

6 Golden Delicious apples
1 tablespoon lemon juice
2 tablespoons flour
$\frac{1}{2}$ teaspoon ground cinnamon
1 jar (11.5 ounces) dulce de leche
2 refrigerated pie crusts (from a 15-
   ounce package)
1 egg, lightly beaten with 1 tablespoon
   water

1. Heat oven to 375°F. Peel, core, and thinly slice the apples, tossing them with the lemon juice as you go so they won't discolor. In a large bowl, toss the sliced apples with flour and cinnamon, then mix with the dulce de leche.

2. Fit one pie crust inside a 10-inch glass pie plate. Top with apple mixture, mounding it high in the center. Moisten the crust edge with a little water and top with the second crust. Pinch edges together to seal. Brush the pie with the egg mixture. Make a few small slits in the top of the pie with a sharp knife.

3. Bake until crust is golden and filling is bubbly, about 1 hour 10 minutes. If crust browns before filling is hot, cover the edges with foil and continue baking. Serve warm or at room temperature.

Glazed Sweet Potato Pie

Candied yams make this the easiest sweet potato pie you'll find.

PREP TIME: 15 MINUTES • BAKE TIME: 40 MINUTES • MAKES: 8 SERVINGS

2 cans (1 pound each) candied yams
    with brown sugar, cinnamon, and
    nutmeg
2 eggs
1 cup half-and-half
1 refrigerated pie crust (from a
    15-ounce package)

1. Heat oven to 375°F. Drain the yams; reserve liquid. In a medium bowl, mash the yams until smooth. Add eggs and half-and-half and whisk well to blend.

2. Fit crust into a 9-inch glass pie plate and pour filling into crust. Bake until center moves only slightly when pan is shaken, 40 to 45 minutes, covering crust with foil if it browns too quickly.

3. Meanwhile, pour liquid from yams into a small saucepan. Bring to a gentle boil and cook until thickened to the consistency of honey and reduced to $1/2$ cup, about 20 minutes. Spread on partially cooled pie.

4. Refrigerate until chilled. Serve cold or at room temperature.

Peach Melba Pie

This pie is delicious by itself. But topping it with vanilla ice cream completes the peach Melba theme and makes it even better.

PREP TIME: 15 MINUTES • COOK TIME: 1 HOUR 15 MINUTES • MAKES: 8 TO 10 SERVINGS

1 bag (16 ounces) frozen sliced
    peaches, defrosted
1 package (10 ounces) frozen
    raspberries in syrup, thawed
3 tablespoons sugar
1 tablespoon cornstarch
2 tablespoons butter
2 refrigerated pie crusts (from a
    15-ounce package)

1. Heat oven to 400°F. In a large bowl, toss together the peaches, raspberries, sugar, and cornstarch.

2. Fit one crust into a 9-inch pie plate. Fill with the peach-berry mixture and dot with butter. Brush the edge of the crust with water and top with the second crust. Pinch edges together to seal and fold the crust under itself. Make a few slits in the center with a sharp knife.

3. Bake 15 minutes, reduce heat to 350°F, and bake until golden and bubbly, about 1 hour longer. Serve warm or at room temperature.

Chocolate Banoffee Pie

Several of the best dessert flavors—banana, chocolate, coffee, and caramel—are here in one delicious pie.

PREP TIME: 15 MINUTES • COOK TIME: 5 MINUTES • CHILL TIME: 30 MINUTES
MAKES: 8 SERVINGS

1 refrigerated pie crust (from a
    15-ounce package)
$\frac{1}{2}$ cup hot fudge sauce
2 bananas, peeled and sliced
1 package (3 ounces) flan mix
$1\frac{3}{4}$ cups milk
$1\frac{1}{2}$ teaspoons instant coffee granules

1. Heat oven to 450°F. Fit crust into a 9-inch pie plate and prick bottom and sides of crust all over with a fork. Bake until golden, 9 to 11 minutes. Cool to room temperature.

2. Spread fudge sauce in the bottom and halfway up the sides of the crust. Top with bananas.

3. Prepare the flan mix according to package directions, using $1\frac{3}{4}$ cups milk, and adding instant coffee granules with milk. Pour over fudge and bananas and chill 30 minutes. Top with syrup from packet included with flan mix. Return to refrigerator and chill completely before serving.

Chocolate Bourbon Pecan Pie

Serve this rich pie with a dollop of fresh whipped cream. There is nothing better.

PREP TIME: 5 MINUTES • **BAKE TIME: 50 MINUTES** • **MAKES: 10 SERVINGS**

1 refrigerated pie crust (from a
    15-ounce package)
3 eggs, slightly beaten
1 1/2 cups chocolate syrup
3/4 cup heavy cream
3 tablespoons bourbon
1 package (6 ounces) pecan pieces
    (1 1/3 cups)

1. Heat oven to 325°F. Fit crust into a 9-inch pie plate.

2. In a large bowl, whisk together the eggs, syrup, cream, and bourbon. Stir in the nuts. Pour filling into pie crust.

3. Bake until filling is puffed and crust is golden, about 50 minutes. Cool in pan on a wire rack to room temperature before serving.

Chocolate-Hazelnut Cream Pie

Be sure that you stir the chocolate hazelnut spread into the pudding while it is still warm to ensure that it is incorporated evenly.

PREP TIME: 5 MINUTES • COOK TIME: 5 MINUTES • CHILL TIME: 3 HOURS

MAKES: 8 SERVINGS

1 shortbread cookie crust (6 ounces)

1 egg white

1 package (3.4 ounces) chocolate pudding mix (not instant)

1¾ cups milk

⅓ cup chocolate-hazelnut spread

1 container (8 ounces) nondairy whipped topping (or 3 cups whipped cream)

2 tablespoons chopped hazelnuts, for garnish

1. Brush crust with egg white and bake according to directions for "golden" crust. Let cool to room temperature.

2. Make pudding according to package directions using the 1¾ cups milk. Stir chocolate-hazelnut spread into hot pudding. Whisk until smooth.

3. Pour pudding into crust and refrigerate until firm, about 3 hours. Top with whipped topping and sprinkle with chopped hazelnuts. Refrigerate until ready to serve. Serve chilled.

Chocolate-Peanut Butter Pie

Like a giant peanut butter cup, these great tastes still taste great together.

PREP TIME: 15 MINUTES   •   COOK TIME: 5 MINUTES   •   MAKES: 10 SERVINGS

1 9-inch Oreo® pie crust

1 egg white

$1/2$ cup chocolate chips

1 package (8 ounces) cream cheese, softened

$1/2$ cup peanut butter

$1 1/2$ cans (14 ounces each) sweetened condensed milk (not evaporated milk)

$1/2$ teaspoon vanilla extract

1 cup confectioners' sugar

1 container (8 ounces) nondairy whipped topping

1. Brush crust with egg white and bake according to package directions for "crisp" crust. Place chocolate chips in a small microwaveproof bowl and heat on 50% power until melted, about 1 minute. Spread melted chocolate over bottom and up the sides of the pie crust. Refrigerate.

2. In a large bowl, combine the cream cheese, peanut butter, condensed milk, and vanilla. Beat with an electric mixer on low speed until creamy. Beat in confectioners' sugar. Fold in whipped topping.

3. Spoon mixture into chilled pie shell. Smooth top. Return to refrigerator and chill completely before serving.

Double Coconut Cream Pie

In case having just coconut filling is not enough for the biggest coconut fans, this pie has a coconut crust as well.

PREP TIME: 15 MINUTES • COOK TIME: 25 MINUTES • MAKES: 8 SERVINGS

3 tablespoons butter, softened
2 1/2 cups sweetened flaked coconut
1 package (3.4 ounces) instant vanilla
    pudding mix
1 can (13.5 ounces) coconut milk,
    chilled
1 container (8 ounces) nondairy
    whipped topping

1. Heat oven to 300°F. Blend together butter and 2 1/4 cups of the coconut with fingers and press evenly onto the bottom and sides of a 9-inch pie pan. Bake until light brown, about 25 minutes. Cool to room temperature.

2. Prepare pudding according to package directions, using 1 can of coconut milk in place of the regular milk in the recipe. Pour filling into shell and refrigerate until firm. Top with whipped topping and remaining 1/4 cup coconut before serving.

Banana Split Pie

Use an ice cream scoop to make this pie. When you cut it, it will be marbled with great colors. Be sure to work fast or the ice cream will melt. If it does, don't worry—just freeze it as quickly as possible.

PREP TIME: 12 MINUTES • FREEZE TIME: 1 HOUR • MAKES: 10 TO 12 SERVINGS

1 shortbread cookie crust (6 ounces)
1 egg white
1 pint chocolate sorbet
¼ cup strawberry squeezable fruit
2 large or 3 small bananas, thinly
   sliced
½ pint vanilla ice cream
1 pint strawberry sorbet
2 tablespoons chocolate syrup

1. Brush crust with egg white and bake according to directions for "golden crust." Let cool to room temperature.

2. Layer bottom of crust with 6 scoops of chocolate sorbet. Drizzle squeezable fruit over and between the scoops. Top with one-fourth of the bananas.

3. Top with 3 scoops vanilla ice cream and another one-fourth of the bananas. Top with scoops of strawberry sorbet, then the chocolate syrup and another one-fourth of the bananas. Top with remaining chocolate sorbet and sprinkle with remaining bananas. Freeze until firm, 1 to 3 hours.

Key Lime Mousse Pie

This delicious light pie is so easy to make, it will become a family favorite in no time.

PREP TIME: 15 MINUTES • COOK TIME: 5 MINUTES • MAKES: 8 SERVINGS

1 graham cracker crust (6 ounces)
1 egg white
1 can (14 ounces) sweetened condensed milk (not evaporated milk)
½ cup limeade concentrate, thawed
1 cup heavy cream

1. Brush crust with egg white and bake according to directions for "golden" crust. Let cool to room temperature.

2. In a large bowl, combine condensed milk and limeade concentrate; stir to mix.

3. In a medium bowl, whip cream until stiff peaks form. Using a rubber spatula, gently fold cream into lime mixture .

4. Pour filling into crust and refrigerate until firm. Serve chilled.

VARIATION

Lemon Mousse Pie
Substitute lemonade concentrate for the limeade concentrate.

S'more Pie

The campfire favorite is transformed into this fun, fabulous pie.

PREP TIME: 10 MINUTES • COOK TIME: 6 MINUTES • MAKES: 10 TO 12 SERVINGS

1 graham cracker crust (6 ounces)

1 egg white

1 package (10 ounces) mini chocolate "kisses"

¾ cup heavy cream

4 whole double graham crackers, crumbled coarsely

16 large marshmallows

1. Brush crust with egg white and bake according to directions for "golden crust." Place chocolate in a small bowl. In a small saucepan, heat cream until almost boiling. Remove from heat and pour over chocolate. Stir until melted.

2. Pour chocolate mixture into crust and sprinkle with graham crackers. Partially stir them in. Refrigerate until firm.

3. Heat broiler. Cut marshmallows in half crosswise. Arrange marshmallow rounds, cut-side down, over the top of the pie in a single layer. Broil pie, 5 inches from heat, until puffed and browned, about 1 minute. Serve warm or at room temperature.

Eggnog Cheesecake Pie

If you like eggnog, you will love this cheesecake.

PREP TIME: 15 MINUTES • COOK/REST TIME: 2 HOURS • MAKES: 10 SERVINGS

1 1/2 packages (8 ounces each) cream
   cheese, at room temperature
1/3 cup granulated sugar
2 eggs
1 cup eggnog
1/2 teaspoon pumpkin pie spice
1 1/2 tablespoons dark rum
1 graham cracker crust (6 ounces)
Confectioners' sugar, for dusting

1. Heat oven to 325°F. In a large bowl, beat cream cheese and sugar with hand mixer on high until smooth and creamy, 5 minutes. Scrape down sides of bowl. Lower mixer speed to medium and beat in eggs one at a time.

2. With the mixer on medium, beat in eggnog, spice, and rum. Place pie crust on baking sheet and pour mixture into crust.

3. Bake until set, about 1 hour. Turn off heat and leave in oven 1 hour longer. Cool to room temperature, then refrigerate until chilled. Dust with confectioners' sugar just before serving.

Berry Marble Cheesecake

This light-as-air cheesecake will soon become a family favorite.

PREP TIME: 20 MINUTES • COOK TIME: 5 MINUTES • CHILL TIME: 1 ½ HOURS

MAKES: 8 SERVINGS

1 graham cracker crust (6 ounces)

1 egg white

1 envelope (.25 ounce) unflavored gelatin

½ cup milk

1 package (8 ounces) cream cheese, softened

⅔ cup sugar

1 tablespoon orange marmalade

¾ cup heavy cream

⅔ cup blueberry pie filling

1. Brush crust with egg white and bake according to directions for "golden" crust. Cool to room temperature.

2. Sprinkle gelatin over milk in a small saucepan. Warm over low heat until dissolved. Cool to room temperature.

3. In a large bowl, combine cream cheese, sugar, and marmalade. With an electric mixer on medium speed, beat until creamy. Switch to low speed and beat in gelatin mixture.

4. In a medium bowl, whip cream until stiff peaks form. Fold it into the filling.

5. Spread cream cheese filling in crust and top with blueberry pie filling. Swirl by making figure eights with a dull knife. Refrigerate until firm, about 1 ½ hours.

Kitchen Sink Candy Pie

This pie has several decadent candy components. Make it for the kids, but you won't be able to resist it yourself.

PREP TIME: 8 MINUTES • COOK TIME: 38 MINUTES • MAKES: 12 SERVINGS

¾ cup sweetened flaked coconut

1½ cups mini marshmallows

1¼ cups chopped pecans

⅔ cup chocolate chips

⅔ cup peanut butter chips

1½ cans (14 ounces each) sweetened condensed milk (not evaporated milk)

1 shortbread cookie crust (6 ounces)

1. Heat oven to 375°F. Place coconut in a square baking pan. Bake 8 minutes until lightly toasted.

2. In a large bowl, combine toasted coconut, marshmallows, pecans, chocolate chips, and peanut butter chips. Stir in condensed milk. Spread mixture evenly in crust.

3. Bake on the bottom rack of the oven 30 minutes. Cool in pan on wire rack to room temperature before serving.

Almond-Peach Pizza

This pretty pizza is perfect for a dessert buffet, cut into small squares.

PREP TIME: 10 MINUTES • COOK TIME: 15 MINUTES • MAKES: 6 TO 10 SERVINGS

1 package (10 ounces) refrigerated
   pizza crust
½ package cream cheese, softened
   (from an 8-ounce package)
1½ tablespoons orange marmalade
1 can (15.25 ounces) sliced peaches
   in heavy syrup, drained
2 tablespoons peach preserves
3 tablespoons sliced almonds

1. Heat oven to 400°F. Unroll the pizza crust and place it on a baking sheet.

2. In a medium bowl, combine cream cheese and orange marmalade. With an electric mixer, blend on low speed until smooth and creamy. Spread cream cheese mixture on crust.

3. Cut each peach slice in half lengthwise. In a small bowl, toss peach slices with peach preserves and arrange them over the crust. Drizzle with juices from the bowl and sprinkle with almonds.

4. Bake until golden, about 15 to 20 minutes. Cool in pan on wire rack and serve warm or at room temperature.

Banana-Chocolate Strudel

Keep phyllo covered as you work. It doesn't matter if the sheets tear as you work. Just be sure that the outside sheet (the one you start with) is whole.

PREP TIME: 10 MINUTES • COOK TIME: 15 MINUTES • MAKES: 4 SERVINGS

6 phyllo sheets (from a 16-ounce
　　package)
$1/2$ stick ($1/4$ cup) butter, melted
2 tablespoons sugar
2 ripe bananas, peeled
$1/3$ cup chocolate chips

1. Heat oven to 425°F. Place one phyllo sheet on a work surface with the short side of the sheet nearest you. Brush with butter and sprinkle evenly with about 1 teaspoon sugar. Top with another phyllo sheet, brushing with butter and sprinkling with sugar. Repeat with remaining phyllo sheets.

2. Starting 3 inches from the side nearest you, arrange the bananas, one just above the other, in the center of the phyllo sheet. Sprinkle chocolate chips over bananas. Then fold the sides of the phyllo toward the center, over the bananas. Next, fold the edge of the phyllo nearest you over the bananas and roll up to form a log.

3. Transfer strudel, seam-side down, to a buttered baking sheet. Cut four (1-inch-long) steam vents diagonally along top of strudel with a sharp knife. Bake until golden, about 15 minutes. Cool on pan at least 10 minutes before serving.

Ginger-Apple Strudel

Don't let this recipe intimidate you—it is so easy to make. Just be bold with the phyllo.

PREP TIME: 20 MINUTES • COOK TIME: 20 MINUTES • MAKES: 6 TO 8 SERVINGS

10 gingersnap cookies

3 tablespoons sugar

8 phyllo sheets (from a 16-ounce package)

1 stick (1/2 cup) butter, melted

1 can (21 ounces) apple pie filling

1. Heat oven to 425°F. In a food processor, grind gingersnaps with sugar to make crumbs. Place one phyllo sheet on a work surface with a long side nearest you. Brush with butter and sprinkle evenly with about 1 1/2 tablespoons of the sugar mixture. Top with another phyllo sheet, brushing with butter and sprinkling with sugar mixture. Repeat with remaining phyllo sheets.

2. Spread apple filling over the center of the stack, 3 inches from the bottom of the sheet and about 2 inches from the sides. Fold sides of phyllo toward the center. Fold bottom edge of phyllo over filling and roll up to form a log.

3. Brush strudel with butter and sprinkle with a bit of additional sugar. Cut four (1-inch-long) steam vents diagonally along top of strudel with a sharp knife.

4. Carefully transfer strudel, seam-side down, to a buttered baking sheet. Bake until golden, about 15 minutes. Cool on pan at least 10 minutes before serving.

Chocolate-Mint Croissants

These are great little treats with a sweet surprise inside.

PREP TIME: 5 MINUTES • COOK TIME: 12 MINUTES • MAKES: 8 SERVINGS

1 package (8 ounces) refrigerated
crescent roll dough
16 rectangular chocolate crème de
menthe thins
1 egg, lightly beaten with 1 tablespoon
water
1 teaspoon sugar

1. Heat oven to 375°F. Carefully unfold crescent roll dough. Tear dough into 8 triangles along perforated lines. Place 2 chocolates at the shortest edge of each triangle and roll up.

2. Brush tops of rolls lightly with egg mixture and sprinkle with sugar. Arrange on ungreased baking sheet. Bake 12 to 15 minutes until puffed and golden. Cool on pan at least 5 minutes before serving.

VARIATION

Almond Crescents
Use 2 teaspoons almond paste or marzipan in each croissant in place of the chocolate mint candies, flattening the almond paste to the shape of the dough and rolling up.

Cherry Cheesecake Turnovers

These perfect turnovers, hot from the oven, make an impressive brunchtime sweet.

PREP TIME: 22 MINUTES • BAKE TIME: 15 MINUTES • MAKES: 4 SERVINGS

1 sheet frozen puff pastry (from a
  17.3-ounce package), thawed
$\frac{1}{2}$ cup (about 4 ounces) cream
  cheese, softened
3 tablespoons sugar
$\frac{1}{2}$ cup cherry pie filling
1 egg, lightly beaten with 1 tablespoon
  water

1. Heat oven to 425°F. Roll out pastry sheet into a 12-inch square on a lightly floured surface. Cut into 4 squares. In a small bowl, combine the cream cheese and sugar. Blend together with a spatula.

2. Put 1$\frac{1}{2}$ tablespoons of the cream cheese mixture in the center of each square. Top with 2 tablespoons pie filling. Brush the edge of each square with water. Fold each square in half to form a triangle. Press the edges together firmly and then fold them to seal securely. Place turnovers on a greased baking sheet.

3. With a sharp knife, cut 3 small slits in the top of each turnover and brush with the egg. Bake until puffed and golden, 12 to 15 minutes. Cool on pan at least 5 minutes before serving.

VARIATION

Blueberry Cheesecake Turnovers
Use blueberry pie filling instead of cherry.

Very Berry Fruit Cups

Use a combination of berries such as raspberries, blackberries, and sliced strawberries for this recipe. Fresh are prettiest, but defrosted frozen berries are still delicious.

PREP TIME: 10 MINUTES • COOK TIME: 25 MINUTES • MAKES: 6 SERVINGS

1 package (10 ounces) frozen puff
   pastry shells, thawed
3 tablespoons raspberry spreadable
   fruit
1 1/2 cups prepared vanilla pudding
2 cups fresh berries

1. Bake puff pastry shells according to package directions. Let cool to room temperature.

2. Spoon spreadable fruit into bottoms of the pastry shells. Top with pudding, then berries. Serve immediately.

Little Chocolate Napoleons

Napkin warning! These little pastries can be messy to eat.

PREP TIME: 15 MINUTES • BAKE TIME: 15 MINUTES • MAKES: 8 SERVINGS

1 sheet frozen puff pastry (from a
    17.3-ounce package), thawed
1 package (2.8 ounces) dark chocolate
    European-style mousse mix
⅔ cup milk
3 tablespoons chocolate syrup
½ cup nondairy whipped topping
Confectioners' sugar, for dusting

1. Heat oven to 400°F. Cut puff pastry along folds into 3 strips. Cut each strip into 4 rectangles. Bake on a baking sheet until golden, 15 minutes. Cool to room temperature.

2. Prepare mousse according to package directions, using ⅔ cup milk.

3. Split each pastry rectangle into 2 layers. Set aside the 8 best-looking pastry tops. Spread each of the remaining layers with ½ teaspoon chocolate syrup, then 1 rounded tablespoon of the mousse, then ½ tablespoon whipped topping. Stack 8 of the mousse-topped layers with the other 8, then add the tops. Refrigerate until chilled. Dust with confectioners' sugar before serving.

Fruitful Finales

Easy Berrymisù

This great dessert is a cross between a tiramisù and a summer pudding. Whatever you call it . . . you will call it delicious.

PREP TIME: 30 MINUTES • CHILL TIME: 2 HOURS • MAKES: 16 SERVINGS

1 package (18.25 ounces) white
    cake mix
1 ⅓ cups plus ¼ cup water
2 tablespoons vegetable oil
3 large egg whites
2 packages (12 ounces each) mixed
    frozen berries
¼ cup orange liqueur
¼ cup water
¾ cup sugar
2 cups heavy cream

1. Bake cake according to package directions, using 1 ⅓ cups water, oil, and egg whites, in a greased 13 x 9-inch glass baking dish. Cool completely.

2. While cake is baking, combine berries, orange liqueur, remaining ¼ cup water, and ½ cup of the sugar. Stir well to slightly break up fruit. Set aside for at least 30 minutes.

3. Poke holes in the cake with a fork or small knife. Spoon berries and juice over cake and refrigerate at least 2 hours for juices to soak into cake.

4. Just before serving, whip heavy cream with remaining ¼ cup sugar. Top cake with cream.

Strawberry Pavlova

Instead of taking the time to bake a large meringue shell, you can make a delicious pavlova using packaged meringue kisses.

PREP TIME: 25 MINUTES • CHILL TIME: 3 HOURS • MAKES: 10 TO 12 SERVINGS

2 cups heavy cream

2 tablespoons sugar

15 large meringue kisses

¼ cup sliced almonds

2 cups sliced strawberries, plus
    additional strawberries for garnish
    (optional)

1. In a medium bowl, whip cream and sugar with a hand mixer on high speed just until firm peaks form.

2. Arrange 8 meringues, flat-side down, on the bottom of an 8-inch glass baking dish. Spread evenly with 1½ cups of the whipped cream.

3. Press 7 meringues, flat-side up, into the cream layer. Spread with 1 cup of the whipped cream and sprinkle with 3 table-spoons of the almonds. Top with a layer of the strawberries. Spread with remaining cream and decorate top with remaining tablespoon of almonds.

4. Chill at least 3 hours. Decorate top with additional strawberries before serving, if desired.

Classic Fruit Trifle

Use canned or thawed frozen mixed fruit or fresh peaches, berries, cherries, or bananas in this classic English dessert.

PREP TIME: 10 MINUTES • CHILL TIME: 3 HOURS • MAKES: 12 SERVINGS

1 prepared all-butter loaf cake
    (12 ounces)
$\frac{1}{3}$ cup seedless raspberry jam
$\frac{1}{2}$ cup sherry
3 cups fruit (fresh, frozen, or
    canned pieces)
2 cups prepared vanilla pudding
$\frac{1}{2}$ cup heavy cream
$\frac{1}{4}$ cup sliced almonds

1. Cut cake into 6 lengthwise slices. Spread 3 slices with jam and sandwich them with remaining slices. Cut each cake strip stack into 5 rectangles.

2. Arrange cake pieces in a 2$\frac{1}{2}$-quart glass bowl. Sprinkle with sherry, top with fruit, then pudding. Chill 3 hours.

3. Just before serving, whip cream until soft peaks form. Top trifle with whipped cream and decorate with sliced almonds.

Fruit Salad Gelatin

When neither fruit salad nor gelatin seems right, this light dessert will be perfect.

PREP TIME: 15 MINUTES • CHILL TIME: 3 HOURS • COOK TIME: 8 MINUTES
MAKES: 4 SERVINGS

¾ cup cranberry juice concentrate
⅓ cup seedless raspberry preserves
¼ cup water
1 package (.25 ounce) unflavored
    gelatin
4 cups fresh fruit (peach slices,
    strawberry halves, banana chunks)
Whipped cream (optional)

1. In a small saucepan, combine juice concentrate, preserves, water, and gelatin. Heat over low heat until gelatin is dissolved. Cool to room temperature, then chill in refrigerator until partially set, about 1 hour.

2. Arrange fruit in four 6- to 8-ounce glasses or one 1½-quart decorative bowl. Pour cranberry mixture over fruit. Chill until set, about 2 hours. Serve with fresh whipped cream, if desired.

Berries in Champagne Jelly

This beautiful dessert will surely impress your guests.

PREP TIME: 8 MINUTES • CHILL TIME: 4½ HOURS • MAKES: 4 SERVINGS

¾ cup white grape juice
½ cup sugar
1 packet (.25 ounce) unflavored
  gelatin
1¼ cups sparkling wine
1½ cups fresh raspberries

1. Combine white grape juice, sugar, and gelatin in a small saucepan. Heat over low heat until dissolved, 2 to 3 minutes.

2. Pour mixture into a bowl and stir in sparkling wine. Chill until partially jelled, about 1½ hours.

3. Gently stir in berries (berries will not float to the top if mixture has been chilled long enough) and spoon mixture into 4 serving glasses. Chill until firm, at least 3 more hours.

Maple-Berry Salad

Balsamic vinegar really brings out the flavor of berries. Serve this salad over angel food cake or pound cake for a pretty and delicious dessert.

PREP TIME: 5 MINUTES • CHILL TIME: 1 HOUR • MAKES: 4 SERVINGS

1 ½ cups frozen strawberries, thawed
2 cups frozen raspberries, thawed
¼ cup maple syrup
1 teaspoon balsamic vinegar

1. Slice strawberries and place in a medium bowl. Add raspberries, syrup, and balsamic vinegar. Gently toss to combine.

2. Cover bowl with plastic wrap and refrigerate for at least 1 hour for flavors to blend.

Tropical Fruit Salad

This refreshing salad is a perfect summertime finale.

PREP TIME: 20 MINUTES • CHILL TIME: 30 MINUTES • MAKES: 4 SERVINGS

1 ripe mango

2 bananas

2 ripe kiwis

1 cup papaya chunks

2 tablespoons frozen limeade
    concentrate, thawed

2 tablespoons chopped stem ginger
    in syrup

1. Peel and slice the mango, bananas, and kiwis into bite-sized pieces and place in a medium bowl. Add papaya chunks.

2. In a small bowl, stir together the limeade concentrate and the stem ginger. Add to the fruit and toss gently. Refrigerate 30 minutes before serving.

Summer Fruit Salad with Honey-Mint Dressing

Use your favorite summer fruits for this recipe: berries, melon, peaches, nectarines . . .

PREP TIME: 15 MINUTES • CHILL TIME: 1 HOUR • MAKES: 4 TO 6 SERVINGS

1 cup vanilla yogurt

2 teaspoons honey

2 teaspoons finely chopped fresh mint

6 cups chilled mixed fresh fruit,
   cut into bite-sized pieces

1. In a small bowl, combine yogurt, honey, and mint. Mix well. Refrigerate at least 1 hour.

2. To serve, place fruit in serving dishes. Drizzle with yogurt dressing.

Tropical Fruit Soup

This pretty soup is perfect when plain sorbet isn't a special enough way to end an elegant summer meal.

PREP TIME: 5 MINUTES • MAKES: 4 SERVINGS

1 pint mango sorbet
1 cup guava nectar
¼ cup lime juice
1 cup coconut sorbet
1 ripe kiwi, peeled and diced

1. Combine mango sorbet, nectar, and lime juice in a blender or food processor. Purée until smooth.

2. Pour soup into four bowls. Place a small scoop of coconut sorbet in each bowl and sprinkle with diced kiwi. Serve immediately.

Spiced Cherry Soup with Cake Croutons

Pound cake "croutons" add a whimsical touch to this lovely cold soup.

PREP TIME: 10 MINUTES • COOK TIME: 20 MINUTES • MAKES: 6 SERVINGS

1 cup mango nectar
1 cup water
¼ cup sugar
1 cinnamon stick
4 whole cloves or 1 whole star anise
1 bag (12 ounces) frozen cherries
5 half-inch-thick slices all-butter loaf
    cake (from a 12-ounce loaf)
6 tablespoons sour cream

1. In a medium saucepan, heat mango nectar, water, sugar, and spices to boiling. Add cherries and simmer until tender, 15 minutes.

2. Cool mixture to room temperature. Remove cinnamon stick and cloves or star anise. Pour cooled mixture into a blender and purée until nearly smooth. Refrigerate until cold.

3. Heat broiler. Cut each loaf cake slice into six 1-inch squares. Broil on foil-lined baking sheet until golden, 4 to 5 minutes, turning once.

4. To serve, spoon soup into serving dishes. Top each with a dollop of sour cream and loaf cake croutons.

Rainbow Fruit Tart

This pretty pastry shop-style dessert is unbelievably simple to make.

PREP TIME: 25 MINUTES • COOK TIME: 20 MINUTES • MAKES: 8 SERVINGS

1 roll (18 ounces) refrigerated sugar
    cookie dough
1½ cups prepared vanilla pudding
4 strawberries, sliced
1 orange, peeled and sliced
1 kiwi, peeled and sliced
1 banana, peeled and sliced
2 tablespoons apricot preserves

1. Heat oven to 350°F. Press sugar cookie dough evenly into the bottom and up the sides of a 10-inch tart pan with a removable bottom.

2. Bake cookie dough until golden, about 20 minutes. Let cool slightly and press down lightly on the center (but not the sides) of the cookie so that crust forms a tart shell. Cool completely.

3. Spread pudding evenly over the bottom of the shell. Arrange sliced fruit in decorative wedges over the pudding.

4. Warm apricot preserves in the microwave just until melted. Force through a small sieve to remove chunks. Brush strained preserves over fruit. Chill until ready to serve.

Two-Sauce Fruit Fondue

This dessert is one of the easiest crowd-pleasers you can imagine.

PREP TIME: 10 MINUTES • COOK TIME: 5 MINUTES • MAKES: 4 SERVINGS

½ cup hot fudge ice cream topping

½ cup heavy cream

½ cup caramel-flavored ice cream
   topping

1 ½ tablespoons each orange, almond,
   coffee, or peppermint liqueur
   (choose two)

Fruit for serving, such as bananas,
   apples, pears, berries

1. In one very small saucepan, combine hot fudge sauce and ¼ cup of the cream. In another very small saucepan, combine caramel sauce and remaining ¼ cup of the cream. Heat each sauce over medium heat, stirring constantly, until warm and blended.

2. Stir a different liqueur into each of the sauces. Serve immediately, either in saucepans or in small wide-mouth crocks, with platters of cut-up fruit and bamboo skewers for dipping.

Double Mango Melba

Better than classic peach Melba. Just be sure that the mangoes are ripe.

PREP TIME: 12 MINUTES • COOK TIME: 2 MINUTES • MAKES: 4 SERVINGS

2 cups frozen raspberries
2 tablespoons sugar
1 pint mango ice cream
2 ripe mangoes, peeled and sliced

1. Heat raspberries and sugar in microwave until thawed, 1 to 2 minutes. Stir gently to mix.

2. Scoop ice cream into four sundae dishes. Top with mango slices and raspberry sauce. Serve immediately.

Rhubarb Fool

You don't have to wait until spring to enjoy this classic rhubarb dessert.

PREP TIME: 15 MINUTES • COOK TIME: 10 MINUTES • CHILL TIME: 1 HOUR

MAKES: 8 SERVINGS

1 package (20 ounces) frozen rhubarb

½ cup water

½ cup sugar

3 tablespoons squeezable strawberry
    fruit spread

1 cup heavy cream

1. In a medium saucepan over medium heat, cook rhubarb, water, and 6 tablespoons of the sugar until the rhubarb is very soft, about 10 minutes.

2. Remove rhubarb mixture from the heat. Stir in fruit spread. Refrigerate until cold, 1 to 2 hours.

3. In a medium chilled bowl, whip the cream with the remaining 2 tablespoons sugar until soft peaks form.

4. Spoon about ¼ cup rhubarb into each of eight 8-ounce glasses, then spoon in a layer of about ¼ cup whipped cream. Repeat, ending with a small dollop of cream. Serve immediately or refrigerate up to 6 hours.

Braised Fruit

This lovely mixture is delicious served over pound cake, angel food cake, or ice cream.

PREP TIME: 5 MINUTES • COOK TIME: 10 MINUTES • MAKES: 4 TO 6 SERVINGS

1 bag (8 ounces) "orchard fruit" mixed dried fruit

1 cup dry white wine (such as Sauvignon Blanc)

2 tablespoons frozen apple juice concentrate, thawed

1 tablespoon butter, melted

1 tablespoon sugar

1 cinnamon stick

1. Heat oven to 400°F. In a small baking dish, combine dried fruit, wine, apple juice concentrate, butter, sugar, and cinnamon stick. Toss lightly to mix.

2. Roast fruit, stirring occasionally, until very soft and slightly golden, 40 minutes. Remove cinnamon stick before serving. Serve warm.

Cranberry-Spice Pears

Serve these pears upright, drizzled with syrup—beautiful!

PREP TIME: 15 MINUTES • COOK TIME: 40 MINUTES • MAKES: 4 SERVINGS

4 Bosc pears, partially ripe
2 cups cranberry juice
3 tablespoons ginger preserves
2 tablespoons sugar
6 peppercorns

1. Using a paring knife, peel and core pears, keeping stems intact. Cut a small slice off the bottom of each pear to make it flat.

2. In a 3-quart saucepan, combine cranberry juice, ginger preserves, sugar, and peppercorns. Bring to a boil and add the pears, laying them sideways in the pan. (The liquid should cover the pears slightly more than halfway.)

3. Simmer pears until tender, about 30 minutes, turning once. Remove pears from pan and chill.

4. Boil remaining liquid until syrupy, about 10 minutes. Remove peppercorns. Serve pears drizzled with syrup.

Winter Fruit Compote

This rich compote is a satisfying cold-weather dessert on its own or a perfect accompaniment to a simple cake.

PREP TIME: 5 MINUTES • **COOK TIME: 30 MINUTES** • **MAKES: 8 SERVINGS**

1 cup orange juice

1 cup water

¼ cup sugar

2 cinnamon sticks, broken in half

1 package (8 ounces) dried figs, halved lengthwise

½ cup dried cranberries

½ teaspoon grated orange zest

1. In a small saucepan, combine orange juice, water, sugar, and cinnamon sticks. Heat to boiling. Reduce heat and simmer until sugar is dissolved.

2. Add figs and cranberries and simmer until figs are soft and liquid is syrupy, about 30 minutes. Add zest and cool to room temperature before serving.

Roasted Pears with Honey and Blue Cheese

When ripe pears are in season, nothing beats this delicious dessert.

PREP TIME: 12 MINUTES • COOK TIME: 20 MINUTES • MAKES: 4 SERVINGS

2 ripe Bartlett pears, cut in half
    lengthwise and cored
1 teaspoon olive oil
5 teaspoons honey
2 teaspoons crumbled blue cheese
2 teaspoons mascarpone cheese

1. Heat oven to 450°F. In a 10-inch glass pie plate, toss pear halves with olive oil. Turn pears cut-side up and drizzle each pear half with ¼ teaspoon honey. Roast until golden, about 20 minutes.

2. In a small bowl, mash together the blue cheese and the mascarpone.

3. To serve, place 1 pear half on each of 4 serving plates. Fill cavities with blue cheese mixture and drizzle with remaining honey. Serve warm.

Roasted Amaretto Peaches

Make these roasted peaches when ripe summer peaches are at their peak.

PREP TIME: 5 MINUTES • COOK TIME: 15 MINUTES • MAKES: 4 SERVINGS

2 large ripe freestone peaches
1 tablespoon butter, melted
⅓ cup sugar
¼ cup water
4 teaspoons almond syrup
4 amaretti cookies, crushed
Crème fraîche (optional)

1. Heat oven to 400°F. Cut peaches in half and remove pits. In a medium bowl, toss peach halves with butter.

2. In the bottom of a 9-inch glass pie plate, combine sugar, water, and almond syrup. Add peaches, cut-side up.

3. Bake, basting occasionally, until tender and golden, 15 to 25 minutes. To serve, place one peach half on each of 4 serving plates. Sprinkle with crushed amaretti cookies. Top with crème fraîche, if desired.

Broiled Figs with Orange-Yogurt Sauce

The simple sweetness of figs is perfectly complemented by the tartness of the sauce.

PREP TIME: 8 MINUTES • COOK TIME: 5 MINUTES • MAKES: 4 SERVINGS

½ cup vanilla yogurt
½ teaspoon grated orange zest
8 fresh figs, halved lengthwise
4 teaspoons light brown sugar

1. Heat broiler. In a small bowl, stir together the yogurt and orange zest.

2. Place figs, cut-side up, on a foil-lined baking sheet. Sprinkle each half with ¼ teaspoon of the sugar. Broil figs 5 inches from heat until bubbly and golden, about 5 minutes.

3. To serve, place 4 fig halves on each of 4 serving plates. Drizzle figs with orange-yogurt sauce.

Butter-Rum Bananas

These bananas are decadent on their own or try them topped with vanilla ice cream or drizzled with heavy cream.

PREP TIME: 5 MINUTES • COOK TIME: 5 MINUTES • MAKES: 4 SERVINGS

3 slightly underripe bananas
⅓ cup (5 tablespoons) butter
1 jar (5 ounces) walnut dessert
   topping in syrup
3 tablespoons spiced rum
Chopped walnuts, for garnish

1. Peel bananas, halve them lengthwise, and halve again crosswise.

2. In a 12-inch skillet, melt butter over medium-high heat. Add half the bananas in one layer and cook until golden, 2 to 3 minutes, turning once. Remove from pan. Repeat with remaining bananas.

3. Stir in walnut topping and rum and cook, stirring, 2 minutes. To serve, divide bananas among 4 serving plates. Drizzle with warm rum sauce and sprinkle with chopped walnuts.

Cinnamon-Glazed Grilled Pineapple

A prepeeled and cored pineapple will make this recipe even easier.

PREP TIME: 15 MINUTES • **COOK TIME: 6 MINUTES** • **MAKES: 4 SERVINGS**

1 fresh ripe pineapple
1 tablespoon cinnamon sugar
8 teaspoons maple syrup

1. Heat broiler. Peel the pineapple and cut into 8 round slices.

2. Place pineapple slices on a foil-lined baking sheet. Sprinkle each with cinnamon sugar and spread with maple syrup.

3. Broil 6 inches from heat until bubbly but not browned, about 6 to 8 minutes. Let cool slightly and serve.

Apricot-Almond Gratin

This crustless tart makes an elegant end to a special meal.

PREP TIME: 10 MINUTES • COOK TIME: 35 MINUTES • MAKES: 8 SERVINGS

½ can (8 ounces) almond paste
   (about ⅓ cup)
⅓ cup sugar
½ stick (¼ cup) softened butter
2 eggs
3 tablespoons flour
2 cans (15.25 ounces each) apricot
   halves in heavy syrup, drained

1. Heat oven to 350°F. In a large bowl, beat together almond paste, sugar, and butter with hand mixer at high speed until creamy. Lower mixer speed to medium and beat in eggs. Using a wooden spoon, stir in flour.

2. Spread almond mixture in a greased 10- to 11-inch (1½-quart) quiche dish. Top with apricot halves.

3. Bake until puffed and slightly golden, 35 to 40 minutes. Serve warm or at room temperature.

VARIATION

Pear-Almond Gratin
Substitute 1 can (29 ounces) pear halves in heavy syrup, drained, for the apricots.

Banana Fritters

Keeping the heat constant is the most difficult part of this recipe. Use a candy/deep-fry thermometer and adjust the heat as necessary as you cook.

PREP TIME: 10 MINUTES • **COOK TIME: 6 MINUTES** • **MAKES: 4 SERVINGS**

4 bananas
1 ½ tablespoons lemon juice
Vegetable oil, for frying
½ cup baking mix
¼ cup milk
1 egg
1 tablespoon granulated sugar
1 teaspoon grated lemon zest
Confectioners' sugar, for dusting

1. Peel bananas and halve lengthwise; sprinkle with lemon juice and set aside.

2. Pour 1 inch of oil into a 9-inch-deep skillet. Heat oil to 370°F. Mix baking mix with milk, egg, sugar, and zest.

3. Dip banana halves in batter and fry two at a time until golden, about 2 minutes per batch. Remove from oil with a slotted spoon and drain fritters on paper towels while frying the remaining batches. Dust with confectioners' sugar just before serving.

Apple Dumplings

Be sure to use small apples for this recipe so that the crust will cover them.

PREP TIME: 25 MINUTES • COOK TIME: 25 MINUTES • MAKES: 4 SERVINGS

2 refrigerated pie crusts
(from a 15-ounce package)
4 peeled and cored Golden Delicious
apples
6 tablespoons firmly packed brown
sugar
2 tablespoons butter
1 teaspoon ground cinnamon
1 egg, lightly beaten

1. Heat oven to 400°F. Cut pie crusts in half. Fold each piece in half to form a triangle. Roll each out so each side of triangle measures 7 inches.

2. Place 1 apple in the center of each triangle. Stuff each with 1½ tablespoons brown sugar and ½ tablespoon butter and sprinkle with ¼ teaspoon cinnamon.

3. Brush dough edges with beaten egg and pinch them together to enclose the apple. Brush outer surface with egg.

4. Bake apples on a baking sheet until golden, 25 to 30 minutes. Serve warm or at room temperature.

Baked Oatmeal Apples

Stuffed baked apples have never been easier. For added richness, serve these with whipped cream.

PREP TIME: 15 MINUTES • **COOK TIME: 40 MINUTES** • **MAKES: 4 SERVINGS**

2 packets (1.62 ounces each)
    cinnamon and spice-flavored
    instant oatmeal
3 tablespoons butter, softened
4 Fuji or Gala apples
¾ cup apple juice

1. Heat oven to 375°F. In a small bowl, combine instant oatmeal and softened butter. Blend together with fingertips.

2. Using a small, sharp knife, carefully core the apples without cutting all the way through to the bottom. Fill them with the oatmeal mixture, pressing it in and forming into a small cap on top.

3. Pour ¾ cup apple juice into a 9-inch glass pie plate. Stand apples in plate.

4. Bake, uncovered, until apples are tender, about 40 minutes, basting once. Place each apple on a serving plate. Serve warm, drizzled with pan juices.

Maple-Apple Pancake

Pancakes don't have to be saved for breakfast only. This giant apple pancake incorporates those great breakfast flavors into a perfect sweet dessert.

PREP TIME: 16 MINUTES • COOK TIME: 24 MINUTES • MAKES: 8 SERVINGS

2 Granny Smith apples, peeled, cored, and sliced
2 tablespoons butter
1 teaspoon lemon juice
¼ teaspoon ground cinnamon
1 cup baking mix
½ cup milk
2 eggs
1 tablespoon sugar
⅓ cup maple syrup

1. Heat oven to 425°F. In a 10-inch ovenproof skillet over medium heat, sauté apples in butter until golden and almost tender, 8 to 10 minutes. Add lemon juice and cinnamon and cook 1 minute longer.

2. In a medium bowl, combine baking mix, milk, eggs, and sugar. Stir until blended. Pour batter over apples in the hot pan and spread with the back of a spoon (don't stir) to cover.

3. Place skillet in the oven and bake until pancake is puffed and golden, 16 to 20 minutes. Drizzle syrup over cake and let cool. Serve warm or at room temperature.

Gingerbread-Apple Bake

Warm spices and apples make this the perfect autumn dessert.

PREP TIME: 20 MINUTES • COOK TIME: 50 MINUTES • MAKES: 12 SERVINGS

6 Golden Delicious apples, peeled,
   cored, and quartered
¼ cup apple juice
¼ cup firmly packed brown sugar
1 tablespoon chopped crystallized
   ginger
1 tablespoon cornstarch
1 package (14 ounces) gingerbread
   cookie and cake mix
1 cup water

1. Heat oven to 350°F. Place apples, apple juice, brown sugar, ginger, and cornstarch in a shallow 2-quart dish. Toss to combine.

2. Prepare gingerbread according to package directions, using the water. Spoon over apples, spreading evenly.

3. Bake until gingerbread is cooked through, about 50 minutes. Serve warm.

Banana Brown Betty

Try serving this great baked dessert with vanilla ice cream or a drizzle of heavy cream.

PREP TIME: 10 MINUTES • COOK TIME: 20 MINUTES • MAKES: 6 SERVINGS

15 gingersnap cookies
½ stick (¼ cup) butter, melted
¼ cup chopped crystallized ginger
6 bananas, peeled and halved
    lengthwise
2 tablespoons sugar
2 tablespoons lemon juice

1. Heat oven to 400°F. Grind ginger-snaps to make 1 cup crumbs. Mix with melted butter and chopped crystallized ginger.

2. Sprinkle ½ cup of the crumbs into a 9-inch glass pie plate. Arrange bananas on top of crumbs and sprinkle with sugar, lemon juice, and remaining crumbs.

3. Bake until golden, 20 to 25 minutes. Serve warm.

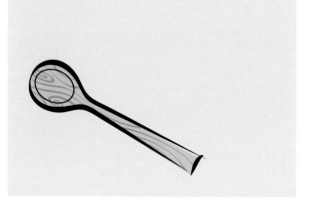

Cherry Clafouti

This classic French dessert is not quite a pudding and not quite a tart. What it is, is delicious.

PREP TIME: 15 MINUTES • COOK TIME: 45 MINUTES • MAKES: 8 SERVINGS

1½ cups heavy cream
¾ cup egg substitute
⅓ cup granulated sugar
1 teaspoon vanilla extract
¼ teaspoon ground cinnamon
⅔ cup flour
1 bag (12 ounces) frozen cherries, thawed
Confectioners' sugar, for dusting

1. Heat oven to 325°F. Whisk together the cream, egg substitute, sugar, vanilla, and cinnamon. Add the flour and stir until just blended. Add the cherries and mix gently.

2. Pour mixture into a buttered 10- to 11-inch (1½-quart) quiche dish. Bake for 45 minutes to 1 hour or until puffed.

3. Let cool slightly and dust top with confectioners' sugar just before serving. Serve warm or at room temperature.

Cornmeal-Crusted Peach Cobbler

Great Southern flavors—corn bread and peaches—mix perfectly in this simple dessert.

PREP TIME: 8 MINUTES • COOK TIME: 35 MINUTES • MAKES: 8 SERVINGS

2 bags (16 ounces each) frozen
   peaches, defrosted
½ cup sugar
¼ cup orange juice
3 tablespoons diced dried apricots
   (about 4 dried apricot halves)
4 teaspoons cornstarch
1 package (8½ ounces) corn muffin
   mix
1 egg
⅓ cup milk

1. Heat oven to 400°F. In a large bowl, combine peaches, sugar, orange juice, dried apricots, and cornstarch. Toss until well combined and spoon into a 9- to 10-inch pie plate.

2. Prepare corn muffin mix according to package directions, using egg and milk. Spoon batter over peaches.

3. Bake until corn bread is cooked through and fruit is bubbly, 35 minutes. Serve warm or at room temperature.

VARIATION

Cornmeal-Crusted Blueberry Cobbler
Substitute 2 bags (12 ounces each) frozen blueberries for peaches and omit the apricots.

Strawberry-Rhubarb Crisp

This classic crowd-pleaser pairs perfectly with a scoop of vanilla ice cream.

PREP TIME: 12 MINUTES • COOK TIME: 30 MINUTES • MAKES: 8 SERVINGS

4 packets (1.62 ounces each)
    "cinnamon and spice"-flavored
    instant oatmeal
1/3 cup chopped walnuts
1/2 cup all-purpose flour
1 stick (1/2 cup) butter, softened
1 bag (20 ounces) frozen rhubarb
1 cup frozen strawberries, thawed and
    cut in half
1 1/4 cups sugar

1. Heat oven to 375°F. In a medium bowl, combine oatmeal, walnuts, and 1/4 cup of the flour. Add butter and blend together with fingers until mixture forms crumbs.

2. In an 11 x 7-inch baking dish, combine rhubarb, strawberries, sugar, and the remaining 1/4 cup of flour; toss. Sprinkle evenly with oatmeal mixture.

3. Bake until bubbly, about 35 to 40 minutes. Serve warm.

VARIATION

Apple-Walnut Crisp
Substitute 5 peeled, cored, and sliced Granny Smith apples and 1/2 cup apple juice for the rhubarb and strawberries. Reduce sugar to 2 tablespoons.

Very Berry Cobbler

This delicious cobbler is topped with premade refrigerated biscuits. It couldn't be easier.

PREP TIME: 10 MINUTES • COOK TIME: 40 MINUTES • MAKES: 8 TO 10 SERVINGS

2 bags (12 ounces each) frozen mixed berries, thawed
½ cup plus 1½ teaspoons sugar
1 tablespoon cornstarch
1 package (12 ounces) refrigerated buttermilk flaky biscuits
2 teaspoons heavy cream

1. Heat oven to 425°F. Toss berries with ½ cup sugar and the cornstarch and spoon into a 2-quart baking dish.

2. Separate biscuits and place on top of berries, spacing 1 inch apart. Brush tops of biscuits with cream and sprinkle with remaining sugar.

3. Bake until tops of biscuits are golden and filling is bubbly, 40 to 45 minutes. If biscuits brown before filling is hot, cover dish loosely with foil and continue baking. Serve warm.

VARIATION

Peach Cobbler
Substitute 2 bags (16 ounces each) frozen peaches for the berries and increase the cornstarch to 4 teaspoons.

Mini Pecan-Blueberry Cobblers

Everyone will love having a personal little cobbler—especially the kids!

PREP TIME: 20 MINUTES • COOK TIME: 20 MINUTES • MAKES: 4 SERVINGS

1 bag (12 ounces) frozen blueberries, thawed
¼ cup sugar
1 tablespoon quick-cooking tapioca
1 cup baking mix
¼ cup milk
¼ cup chopped pecans
½ teaspoon grated lemon zest

1. Heat oven to 425°F. In a medium bowl, toss blueberries with 2 tablespoons of the sugar and the tapioca. Set aside for 15 minutes.

2. In another medium bowl, stir together the baking mix, milk, pecans, lemon zest, and the remaining 2 tablespoons sugar. Knead just until well blended.

3. Spoon berries into six 5- to 6-ounce ramekins. Roll dough into 6 balls, flatten them slightly, and place over berries.

4. Place ramekins on a baking sheet and bake until the crusts are golden and the fruit is bubbly, 20 to 25 minutes. Serve warm or at room temperature.

Peach Bruschettas

These bruschettas are crisp and fruity, like small tarts that can be made in minutes.

PREP TIME: 10 MINUTES • COOK TIME: 30 MINUTES • MAKES: 4 SERVINGS

8 slices (¾ inch thick) rustic Italian
    bread
8 teaspoons butter, softened
8 teaspoons apricot spreadable fruit
8 "harvest spice"-flavored peach
    slices (from a 15-ounce can)
4 teaspoons sugar
Crème fraîche, for serving (optional)

1. Heat oven to 375°F. Spread both sides of bread with butter, dividing evenly. Spread one side with apricot spreadable fruit.

2. Cut each peach slice in half lengthwise. Arrange on top of jam and sprinkle with sugar.

3. Place bruschettas on a baking sheet and bake until fruit is cooked and bread is crusty and golden, about 30 minutes. Cool to room temperature. Serve with crème fraîche, if desired.

VARIATION

Apricot Bruschettas
Substitute 8 apricot halves for the peach slices.

Spoon Sweets

Frozen Mixed Berry Mousse

You can prepare this beautiful mousse in one large freezerproof bowl, if you prefer. Either way, your guests or your family will be impressed and delighted.

PREP TIME: 15 MINUTES • COOK TIME: 5 MINUTES • FREEZE TIME: 3 HOURS
MAKES: 4 SERVINGS

1 package (12 ounces) frozen mixed berries
1 cup sugar
1 packet (.25 ounce) unflavored gelatin
1 cup heavy cream

1. In a small saucepan, combine berries and sugar. Using a potato masher, crush berries into sugar. Bring mixture to a boil, reduce heat, and simmer over medium heat until soft, about 5 minutes.

2. In a blender, combine 1 ½ cups of the warm berry mixture and the gelatin. Blend on low speed for 1 minute. Using a rubber spatula, press mixture through a sieve and refrigerate until cool to the touch, about 10 minutes. Reserve remaining ½ cup berry mixture.

3. In a medium bowl, whip cream until stiff. Fold into fruit-gelatin mixture. Spoon into four 8-ounce serving glasses and freeze until firm, at least 3 hours. Serve topped with reserved berry sauce.

Five-Minute Chocolate Mousse

This mousse shouldn't even take five minutes to make. It's the easiest way to impress your guests or treat your family without any fuss.

PREP TIME: 5 MINUTES • MAKES: 4 SERVINGS

2 cups nondairy whipped topping
2 cups prepared chocolate pudding
½ cup chocolate syrup
Grated chocolate, for garnish

1. In a medium bowl, combine whipped topping, pudding, and chocolate syrup. Very gently fold ingredients together, using a rubber spatula, until almost blended but still streaky.

2. Spoon into serving glasses. Refrigerate until ready to serve. Sprinkle with grated chocolate just before serving.

White Chocolate-Amaretto Mousse

This elegant dessert is worthy of being served to dinner guests.

PREP TIME: 15 MINUTES • CHILL TIME: 1 HOUR • MAKES: 4 SERVINGS

1 cup white chocolate chips
1²⁄₃ cups heavy cream
¹⁄₃ cup amaretto liqueur
2 tablespoons light corn syrup
8 amaretti cookies, crushed

1. Place chocolate chips in a medium bowl. In a small saucepan, heat ¹⁄₃ cup of the cream and the amaretto until almost boiling. Pour cream mixture over chocolate chips and stir until chocolate is melted and smooth. Stir in corn syrup. Refrigerate just until cool to the touch, about 20 minutes.

2. In a large bowl, beat remaining 1¹⁄₃ cups cream until stiff. Stir about one-fourth of the whipped cream into the chocolate mixture just until blended. Fold in remaining cream.

3. Spoon half the mousse in 4 glasses, dividing evenly. Sprinkle with half the crushed cookies. Top with the remaining mousse.

4. Refrigerate 1 hour and sprinkle with remaining cookies just before serving.

Mocha Mousse

You can also garnish this fluffy mousse with whipped cream, grated chocolate, or chocolate cookie crumbs.

PREP TIME: 12 MINUTES • CHILL TIME: 3 TO 4 HOURS • MAKES: 4 SERVINGS

¾ cup semisweet chocolate chips
½ cup milk
2 teaspoons instant coffee powder
1 cup marshmallow creme dessert
　　topping
1 cup heavy cream
Chocolate-covered coffee beans, for
　　garnish (optional)

1. Place chocolate chips in a large bowl. In a small saucepan, heat milk and coffee powder until almost boiling. Pour over chocolate and stir until smooth and no longer hot. Add marshmallow creme and stir gently to blend.

2. In a medium bowl, beat cream until stiff. Fold cream into chocolate mixture in three additions.

3. Spoon mousse into 6 serving glasses and refrigerate until firm, 3 to 4 hours. Serve chilled. Garnish with chocolate-covered coffee beans, if desired.

Chestnut Coupe

This elegant classic dessert is so simple to make any time.

PREP TIME: 12 MINUTES • MAKES: 6 SERVINGS

¾ cup heavy cream
2 tablespoons dark rum
1 can (17.5 ounces) chestnut spread
½ cup grated bittersweet chocolate

1. In a large bowl, whip cream until soft peaks form.

2. In a separate bowl, whisk rum into chestnut spread. Spoon 1 tablespoon of the mixture into each of 6 serving glasses.

3. Fold cream into the remaining chestnut spread. Spoon the cream mixture over rum mixture and sprinkle with grated chocolate. Refrigerate until ready to serve.

Lemon Rice Pudding

Homemade rice pudding couldn't be faster to make.

PREP TIME: 5 MINUTES • COOK TIME: 20 MINUTES • CHILL TIME: 2 HOURS

MAKES: 4 SERVINGS

3 cups milk

1 cup instant white rice

¼ cup sugar

¼ cup lemon curd

1 teaspoon grated lemon zest
  (optional)

1. In a medium saucepan, bring milk, rice, and sugar just to a boil. Reduce heat and simmer 20 minutes, stirring occasionally until slightly thickened.

2. Transfer mixture to a bowl, cover with plastic wrap, and chill until thoroughly cool, about 2 hours.

3. Swirl lemon curd into cooled pudding. Spoon pudding into serving glasses and top with grated lemon zest, if desired.

VARIATION

Chocolate Rice Pudding

Substitute 2 tablespoons chocolate syrup for the lemon curd and omit the lemon zest. Garnish with grated chocolate, if desired.

Coconut Rice Pudding

You can serve this with fresh sliced mango or pineapple slices. Be sure not to use "converted" rice for this recipe.

PREP TIME: 5 MINUTES • COOK TIME: 25 MINUTES • MAKES: 4 SERVINGS

½ cup raw long-grain white rice
1 can (13.5 ounces) regular or "lite" coconut milk
1¼ cups milk
¼ cup sugar
⅛ teaspoon salt
½ teaspoon vanilla extract
⅓ cup sweetened flaked coconut

1. Heat oven to 350°F. In a 3-quart saucepan, combine rice, coconut milk, milk, sugar, and salt. Bring to a boil over medium heat, reduce heat to low, and simmer until rice is tender and pudding is somewhat thickened, 25 to 30 minutes.

2. Meanwhile, place flaked coconut in a small baking dish and bake just until the edges are lightly browned, 7 minutes.

3. Transfer pudding to a bowl, cover with plastic wrap, and chill. Spoon pudding into serving glasses and sprinkle with toasted coconut.

Sweet 'n' Spicy Polenta Pudding

This warm pudding is a perfect comfort food for a cold winter night.

PREP TIME: 10 MINUTES • COOK TIME: 5 MINUTES • MAKES: 4 TO 6 SERVINGS

3 tablespoons raisins

3 tablespoons sherry or brandy

½ package (8.8 ounces) instant polenta (⅔ cup)

1¾ cups water

½ teaspoon salt

½ cup mascarpone cheese, softened

¼ cup firmly packed light brown sugar

¼ teaspoon pumpkin pie spice

¼ cup sliced almonds

1. In a small saucepan, combine raisins and sherry and heat until boiling. Remove from heat and let stand 10 minutes.

2. Cook polenta according to package directions using water and salt. Immediately add sherry mixture, mascarpone, sugar, and spice. Stir quickly to combine.

3. Spoon warm pudding into serving dishes. Sprinkle with almonds and serve immediately.

Eggnog Bread Pudding

A perfect dish for a morning get-together during the holidays.

PREP TIME: 15 MINUTES • COOK TIME: 35 MINUTES • MAKES: 6 SERVINGS

1 loaf (1 pound) cinnamon-raisin bread
1½ tablespoons softened butter, plus
    more for buttering casserole dish
2½ cups eggnog
3 tablespoons sugar
4 eggs
Confectioners' sugar, for dusting

1. Heat oven to 350°F. Arrange bread on baking sheets and toast until golden, turning once. Lightly spread one side of each slice with butter. Cut crusts from bread and cut slices in half diagonally.

2. In a large bowl, whisk together the eggnog, sugar, and eggs.

3. Arrange bread in a buttered 1½-quart casserole. Top with egg mixture. Gently press down on bread with the back of a wooden spoon to saturate.

4. Bake until puffed and golden, 35 to 40 minutes. Just before serving, dust with confectioners' sugar. Serve warm.

Double Chocolate Bread Pudding

This chocolate bread pudding is perfect for kids and adults alike.

PREP TIME: 10 MINUTES • COOK TIME: 1 HOUR 10 MINUTES • MAKES: 10 SERVINGS

4 eggs
2½ cups half-and-half
¾ cup chocolate syrup
1 teaspoon vanilla extract
1 prepared chocolate-marbled butter
    loaf cake (12 ounces)
Confectioners' sugar, to garnish

1. Heat oven to 325°F. In a large bowl, whisk together the eggs, half-and-half, chocolate syrup, and vanilla.

2. Cut loaf cake in half lengthwise, and slice halves into ½-inch slices. Arrange slices, overlapping edges, in a shallow 2-quart rectangular baking dish. Pour egg mixture over cake slices.

3. Bake until puffed and golden, about 1 hour 10 minutes. Just before serving, dust with confectioners' sugar. Serve warm or at room temperature.

Warm Strawberry Soufflés

Did you ever think soufflé could be this easy to make? Don't be intimidated by the foil cuff—it is simpler to make than you might imagine.

PREP TIME: 15 MINUTES • BAKE TIME: 22 MINUTES • MAKES: 4 SERVINGS

2 tablespoons sugar, plus more for
　　dusting
3 egg whites
¼ teaspoon cream of tartar
Pinch salt
¾ cup squeezable strawberry spread

1. Heat oven to 400°F. Fold each of four 14 x 12-inch strips of foil in thirds lengthwise (they should be about 4 inches by 14 inches) and wrap around four 5- to 6-ounce ramekins. Overlap and crimp edges to secure. (The foil cuffs will be taller than the ramekins.) Spray insides of ramekins and foil with nonstick cooking spray and dust with sugar, shaking out excess.

2. In a large bowl, beat egg whites, 2 tablespoons sugar, cream of tartar, and salt with an electric mixer on medium speed until firm peaks form.

3. Place squeezable fruit in a medium bowl. Stir in one-fourth of the beaten egg whites. Using a rubber spatula, gently fold in remaining egg whites.

4. Spoon into ramekins and bake until puffed and slightly golden, 20 to 22 minutes. Carefully remove foil cuffs and serve immediately.

Mexican Chocolate Soufflés

These oh-so-easy soufflés have a touch of spice and taste as special as they look.

PREP TIME: 15 MINUTES • BAKE TIME: 22 MINUTES • MAKES: 4 SERVINGS

2 tablespoons sugar, plus more for
   dusting
3 egg whites
¼ teaspoon cream of tartar
Pinch salt
¾ cup chocolate syrup
¼ teaspoon ground cinnamon
Pinch ground cayenne pepper

1. Heat oven to 400°F. Fold each of four 14 x 12-inch strips of foil in thirds lengthwise (they should be about 4 inches by 14 inches) and wrap around four 7- to 8-ounce ramekins. Overlap and crimp edges to secure. (The foil cuffs will be taller than the ramekins.)

Spray insides of ramekins and foil with nonstick cooking spray and dust with sugar, shaking out excess.

3. In a large bowl, beat egg whites, 2 tablespoons sugar, the cream of tartar, and salt with a hand mixer until the mixture forms firm peaks.

3. In a medium bowl, combine chocolate syrup, cinnamon, and cayenne. Stir in one-fourth of the beaten egg whites. Using a rubber spatula, gently fold in remaining egg whites.

4. Spoon into ramekins and bake until puffed and slightly golden, 20 to 22 minutes. Carefully remove foil cuffs and serve immediately.

Triple Chocolate Parfait

Use a vegetable peeler to shave chocolate from a bar of white chocolate.

PREP TIME: 10 MINUTES • MAKES: 4 SERVINGS

5 chocolate wafer cookies
2 cups prepared chocolate pudding
¼ cup shaved white chocolate

1. Place chocolate cookies in the bowl of a food processor. Pulse processor to make crumbs.

2. Spoon 1 tablespoon crumbs into bottom of each of 4 glass goblets. Top each with ½ cup chocolate pudding and garnish each with 1 tablespoon shaved white chocolate. Serve immediately.

Banana Cream Pie Parfait

All of the flavors of banana cream pie and no cooking required!

PREP TIME: 12 MINUTES • MAKES: 4 SERVINGS

1 cup graham cracker crumbs
2 cups prepared vanilla pudding
4 bananas, peeled and sliced
2 cups nondairy whipped topping

In each of four 16-ounce goblets, layer
¼ cup of the graham cracker crumbs,
½ cup pudding, 1 sliced banana, and
½ cup whipped topping. Sprinkle each
with a pinch more crumbs for garnish.
Serve immediately.

VARIATION

Chocolate Banana Cream Pie Parfait
Grind 20 chocolate wafer cookies to make
1 cup crumbs. Substitute for graham
cracker crumbs. For **Double Chocolate
Banana Cream Parfait,** substitute chocolate pudding for the vanilla pudding as
well as the chocolate cookie crumbs.

Tres Leches

This traditional Latin dessert is called tres leches because it uses three milk products.

PREP TIME: 15 MINUTES • **CHILL TIME: 4 HOURS** • **MAKES: 10 SERVINGS**

1 prepared all-butter loaf cake
    (12 ounces)
1 can (12 ounces) evaporated skim
    milk
½ cup dulce de leche
2 tablespoons rum
1 cup heavy cream

1. Slice loaf cake into 8 slices. Arrange slices to cover the bottom of a 6 x 10-inch baking dish (you will have to cut one slice into thirds and squeeze it in). Pour evaporated milk over the cake.

2. In a medium chilled bowl, combine dulce de leche and rum. Using a hand mixer on low speed, mix until blended. Add cream and whip on high speed until firm peaks form.

3. Spoon cream mixture evenly over soaked cake. Refrigerate 4 hours before serving. Serve chilled.

Chocolate Tiramisù

A delicious and easy version of the Italian classic. It is best if chilled overnight, so prepare it the day before serving and make dinner party day even easier.

PREP TIME: 25 MINUTES • COOK TIME: 2 MINUTES • CHILL TIME: 6 HOURS
MAKES: 12 SERVINGS

3 cups heavy cream
1 cup chocolate chips
¾ cup coffee
½ cup coffee-flavored liqueur
1 package (7 ounces) savoiardi
   biscuits (ladyfingers)
1 envelope powdered chocolate drink
   mix, for dusting

1. In a medium saucepan, heat heavy cream until almost boiling. Place chocolate chips in a large bowl. Pour cream over chocolate chips. Stir until smooth and chill until cold, about 1 hour.

2. In a large bowl, whip the chilled cream mixture with an electric mixer on medium speed until just stiff.

3. In a small bowl, stir together coffee and liqueur. One at a time, dip half the biscuits into the coffee mixture and arrange in a single layer to cover the bottom of a 10-inch-square glass baking dish. Spread with half the cream. Repeat layers with the remaining biscuits, coffee mixture, and cream mixture.

4. Refrigerate at least 6 hours. To serve, sprinkle top with chocolate drink mix, cut into squares, and place on serving plates.

Coconut Flan

This impressive dessert is perfect for last-minute guests.

PREP TIME: 10 MINUTES • COOK TIME: 10 MINUTES • CHILL TIME: 2 HOURS

MAKES: 8 SERVINGS

1 tablespoon coconut rum (optional)
1 package (5.5 ounces) flan
   (Spanish-style custard) mix
1 can (13.5 ounces) lite coconut milk
2½ cups milk
¼ cup sweetened flaked coconut

1. In a small bowl, stir coconut rum into contents of caramel packet (included in flan mix). Spoon mixture into eight ½-cup ramekins or pudding cups. (If you're not using the rum, use the plain caramel in the ramekins.)

2. Prepare flan mix according to package directions, substituting the coconut milk and 2½ cups milk for the milk on package directions. Pour custard into prepared ramekins. Refrigerate until firm, 2 to 3 hours.

3. Heat oven to 350°F. Place flaked coconut in a 9-inch baking pan and toast until fragrant, 8 to 10 minutes.

4. To serve, invert custard onto serving dishes and sprinkle with toasted coconut.

VARIATION

Chocolate Flan
Substitute 4 cups chocolate milk for the milk and coconut milk. Use bourbon or coffee liqueur for the coconut rum.

Chocolate-Hazelnut Semifreddo

Chocolate and hazelnuts are a classically Italian flavor combination.

PREP TIME: 10 MINUTES • FREEZE TIME: 6 HOURS • MAKES: 10 SERVINGS

1 cup hazelnuts
2 packages (8 ounces each) cream
   cheese, softened
1¼ cups sugar
⅔ cup chocolate chips
1 tablespoon orange marmalade
1¾ cups half-and-half

1. Heat oven to 350°F. Place hazelnuts in a small baking pan and toast until fragrant, about 12 minutes, shaking pan occasionally. Cool to room temperature.

2. In the bowl of a food processor, combine cream cheese, sugar, chocolate chips, marmalade, and hazelnuts. With machine running, slowly add half-and-half, processing until almost smooth.

3. Pour mixture into a 1½-quart loaf pan lined with plastic wrap.

4. Cover and freeze until firm, 6 hours or overnight. To serve, invert pan onto large plate and pull edges of plastic wrap to lift off pan and release semifreddo. Cut into slices and serve immediately.

Pumpkin-Pecan Terrine

This easy terrine is a perfect Thanksgiving alternative to pumpkin pie.

PREP TIME: 20 MINUTES • FREEZE TIME: 5 HOURS • MAKES: 8 SERVINGS

14 gingersnap cookies

½ cup pecan pieces

2 tablespoons chopped crystallized
    ginger

2 pints super-premium vanilla ice
    cream, slightly softened

1 cup pumpkin pie mix (from a
    30-ounce can)

1. In the bowl of a food processor, combine gingersnaps, pecans, and ginger. Process to make crumbs.

2. In a large bowl, fold 1 pint of the ice cream into the pumpkin pie mix, working quickly to avoid melting the ice cream too much.

3. Pat 1¼ cups of the ginger crumbs onto the bottom of a 1½-quart loaf pan lined with plastic wrap. (Make sure edges of plastic wrap hang over edges of pan.) Spread pumpkin-ice cream mixture on top. Sprinkle with remaining crumbs and top with remaining vanilla ice cream. Freeze until firm, 4 to 5 hours.

4. To serve, invert pan onto large plate and pull edges of plastic wrap to lift off pan and release terrine. Cut into slices and serve immediately.

Butter Pecan Panna Cotta

This delicate dessert is an elegant way to end a special meal.

PREP TIME: 20 MINUTES • CHILL TIME: 6 HOURS • MAKES: 4 SERVINGS

1 cup milk
2¼ teaspoons unflavored gelatin
1 pint super-premium butter pecan ice
    cream, softened
4 teaspoons blueberry spreadable
    fruit

1. Lightly brush four 7-ounce ramekins or custard cups with oil and chill until ready to use.

2. In a medium saucepan, heat milk until warm. Sprinkle with gelatin and stir over very low heat until gelatin dissolves completely, about 10 minutes. Whisk in ice cream. Pour into ramekins and refrigerate until set, about 6 hours.

3. To serve, run a small knife around edge of ramekins and invert onto serving plates. Tap bottoms of ramekins gently to release. Serve each with a small spoonful of spreadable fruit on the side.

VARIATION

Coffee Panna Cotta
Substitute coffee ice cream for the butter pecan, and raspberry spreadable fruit for the blueberry.

Frozen "Hot" Chocolate

The flavor of hot chocolate with marshmallows doesn't have to be saved for wintertime. This iced confection is perfect all year-round.

PREP TIME: 5 MINUTES • COOK TIME: 5 MINUTES • FREEZE TIME: 2½ HOURS
MAKES: 4 SERVINGS

4 cups milk
6 packets (1 ounce each) instant hot chocolate mix
½ cup marshmallow creme dessert topping, plus more for garnish

1. In a medium saucepan, heat milk to almost boiling. Add hot chocolate mix and stir well. Cool slightly. Pour mixture into a square metal baking pan. Freeze until almost firm, 2 to 3 hours, stirring mixture with a fork every 30 minutes.

2. Stir in marshmallow creme, leaving some lumps. Refreeze until firm.

3. Spoon into glass mugs. Top with additional marshmallow creme, if desired, and serve immediately.

Affogato al Caffe

This delicious simple dessert combines after-dinner coffee and ice cream. Have guests pour the hot espresso over the ice cream at the table.

PREP TIME: 3 MINUTES • MAKES: 4 SERVINGS

1 ½ tablespoons instant espresso
    powder
½ cup boiling water
1 pint vanilla ice cream

1. In a liquid measuring cup, combine instant espresso powder with ½ cup boiling water. Mix well. Divide espresso among 4 espresso cups, or pour into a small pitcher or sauceboat.

2. Place 1 large scoop of ice cream in each of 4 coffee cups. Top each with hot espresso. Serve immediately.

VARIATIONS

Chocolate Affogato al Caffe
Substitute chocolate ice cream for the vanilla.

Caramel Affogato al Caffe
Substitute dulce de leche ice cream for the vanilla.

Black-and-White Milkshake

Can't decide between chocolate and vanilla? This milkshake is the ultimate solution.

PREP TIME: 5 MINUTES • MAKES: 2 SERVINGS

6 chocolate sandwich cookies
2 cups vanilla ice cream
1 ½ cups milk
2 tablespoons chocolate syrup

1. Crumble cookies into the blender container. Pulse blender to chop cookies into crumbs.

2. Add ice cream, milk, and chocolate syrup. Pulse blender until combined and creamy. Serve immediately.

Mandarin-Campari Granita

A grown-up way to end a summer meal.

PREP TIME: 5 MINUTES • FREEZE TIME: 8 HOURS • MAKES: 4 SERVINGS

2 cans (11 ounces each) mandarin
    orange segments in light syrup
¼ cup Campari® liqueur

1. Freeze unopened cans for at least 8 hours.

2. Soak unopened cans in hot water for 2 minutes. Open cans and pour juices into the bowl of a food processor. Cut fruit into 2-inch pieces, and add to juices. Add Campari and purée just until smooth. Refreeze until firm, if necessary. Serve immediately or transfer to a plastic container and store in the freezer.

Melon-Lime Granita

You can make this simple granita with any melon you like. Just be sure it's ripe.

PREP TIME: 12 MINUTES • FREEZE TIME: 3 HOURS • MAKES: 4 TO 6 SERVINGS

½ cup water
¼ cup sugar
⅓ cup frozen limeade concentrate
4 cups ripe honeydew melon chunks

1. In a small saucepan, combine water and sugar. Heat over medium heat just to boiling, stirring constantly. Stir until sugar is dissolved. Remove pan from heat and add limeade.

2. In the bowl of a food processor, combine sugar mixture and melon. Purée until smooth.

3. Transfer mixture to a square metal baking pan and place in freezer. Freeze until firm, about 3 hours, stirring with a fork every half hour. Serve immediately or transfer to a plastic container and store in the freezer.

Caramel-Pear Sorbet

The sweet tastes of pears and caramel blend perfectly in this super-easy sorbet.

PREP TIME: 5 MINUTES • FREEZE TIME: 9 HOURS • MAKES: 4 TO 6 SERVINGS

2 cans (15.25 ounces each) sliced
    pears in heavy syrup
5 tablespoons dulce de leche

1. Freeze unopened cans of pears for at least 8 hours.

2. Soak unopened cans in hot water for 2 minutes. Open cans and pour juices into the bowl of a food processor. Cut fruit into 2-inch pieces and add to juices. Add dulce de leche and purée just until smooth.

3. Transfer mixture to square metal baking pan. Refreeze until firm, about 1 hour, and purée again until smooth. Serve immediately or transfer to a plastic container and store in the freezer.

Ginger-Peach Sorbet

This instant sorbet is delicious and delicately flavored. And because it is made with canned peaches, you don't need to wait for peach season to serve it.

PREP TIME: 5 MINUTES • FREEZE TIME: 8 HOURS • MAKES: 4 TO 6 SERVINGS

2 cans (15¼ ounces each)
    peaches in heavy syrup
4 teaspoons ginger preserves

1. Freeze unopened cans for at least 8 hours.

2. Soak unopened can in hot water for 2 minutes. Open can and pour juices into the bowl of a food processor. Cut fruit into 2-inch pieces and add to juices. Add preserves and purée just until smooth. Serve immediately or transfer to a plastic container and store in the freezer.

VARIATION

Raspberry Peach Sorbet
Substitute 1 tablespoon raspberry syrup for the ginger preserves.

Sorbet Sundae

This simple sundae has no fat, but lots of flavor and style. Use the most interesting flavors of juice concentrate, like passion fruit or cranberry-grape.

PREP TIME: 10 MINUTES • MAKES: 4 SERVINGS

1 pint fruit sorbet
1 cup diced fresh fruit or berries
½ cup fruit juice concentrate,
    defrosted

1. Scoop fruit sorbet into 4 serving dishes.

2. Top each serving with ¼ cup fruit and 2 tablespoons defrosted fruit juice concentrate. Serve immediately.

Banana Colada Ice Cream

For banana lovers only!! This rich ice cream is made without an ice-cream maker.

PREP TIME: 5 MINUTES • FREEZE TIME: 3 HOURS • MAKES: 4 TO 6 SERVINGS

3 ripe bananas, peeled
6 tablespoons frozen piña colada mix
½ cup heavy cream

1. In the bowl of a food processor, combine bananas, piña colada mix, and cream. Purée until smooth. Pour mixture into a square metal baking pan and freeze until firm, about 3 hours, stirring every 30 minutes with a fork.

2. Scoop ice cream into a plastic container and store in the freezer until ready to serve. Purée again before serving, if necessary.

Lemonade Swirl Ice Cream

This is a pretty and refreshing alternative to regular ice cream.

PREP TIME: 15 MINUTES • **FREEZE TIME: 2 HOURS** • **MAKES: 4 SERVINGS**

1 half gallon super-premium vanilla ice
cream, frozen solid
1 ⅓ cups frozen pink lemonade
concentrate

1. Run hot water on the outside of the carton of ice cream for 30 seconds. Squeeze the block of ice cream out of the carton onto work surface. Cut the ice cream into 5 horizontal slices, working from bottom to top, with a chef's knife. (You will have to dip your knife in hot water between each cut.)

2. Rebuild the block of ice cream in the carton, spreading ⅓ cup lemonade concentrate between each layer.

3. Cover the top of the ice cream with plastic wrap and refreeze until solid, about 2 hours. To serve, spoon ice cream into serving dishes using an ice cream scoop, making sure to scoop through layers so ice cream is swirled.

Nut Lover's Ice Cream

The flavor you always dreamed of!

PREP TIME: 10 MINUTES • COOK TIME: 8 MINUTES • FREEZE TIME: 1 HOUR
MAKES: 8 SERVINGS

½ cup finely chopped pecans
½ cup sweetened flaked coconut
½ cup honey-roasted peanuts
2 pints vanilla ice cream, slightly
   softened

1. Heat oven to 350°F. Place pecans and coconut in a square baking pan and toast, stirring halfway through cooking, until fragrant, 8 to 10 minutes.

2. Transfer toasted pecans and coconut to a large bowl, and let cool to room temperature. Crumble coconut with fingers.

3. Finely chop honey-roasted nuts and add to pecans and coconut.

4. Stir nut mixture into ice cream. Refreeze until firm, about 1 hour. Serve immediately or transfer to a plastic container and store in the freezer.

VARIATION

Try other nut combinations. For a more sophisticated flavor, use honey-roasted mixed nuts instead of the peanuts and sliced almonds for the pecans.

Chocolate-Hazelnut Sundae

You can make this sundae using the microwave, if you like, by combining the cream and spread in a medium bowl and heating. Just watch carefully that it doesn't overflow.

PREP TIME: 12 MINUTES • COOK TIME: 2 MINUTES • MAKES: 4 SERVINGS

½ cup heavy cream
¼ cup chocolate-hazelnut spread
1 pint super-premium chocolate ice cream
¼ cup chopped hazelnuts

1. In a small saucepan, heat ¼ cup of the heavy cream until almost boiling. Remove from heat. Add chocolate-hazelnut spread and stir until smooth.

2. In a small bowl, beat remaining cream just until stiff.

3. Scoop ice cream into 4 serving dishes. Drizzle each sundae with chocolate-hazelnut sauce, sprinkle with chopped nuts, and top each with a dollop of whipped cream.

Chocolate-Mint Sundae

It's fun to serve this sundae with a pink-and-white-striped peppermint stick for garnish. For a more sophisticated look, use a mint sprig.

PREP TIME: 8 MINUTES • MAKES: 4 SERVINGS

½ cup chocolate syrup
¾ teaspoon mint extract
6 starlight mint candies
1½ pints chocolate ice cream
4 peppermint sticks or mint sprigs,
   for garnish

1. In a small bowl, stir together the chocolate syrup and the mint extract. Unwrap the candies and place them in a sealable plastic bag. With a mallet or the bottom of a saucepan, crush the candies into crumbs.

2. Scoop ice cream into 4 serving dishes. Drizzle with chocolate-mint syrup and sprinkle with crumbled candies. Garnish as desired. Serve immediately.

VARIATION

Peppermint-Chocolate Sundae
Substitute peppermint ice cream for the chocolate ice cream.

Sunset Citrus Pops

Because freezer temperatures differ, you should start checking the pops after one hour.

PREP TIME: 5 MINUTES • FREEZE TIME: 4 HOURS • MAKES: 8 SERVINGS

¼ cup grenadine syrup
¾ cup lemonade
1 cup orange juice

1. Stir grenadine into lemonade. Fill eight 2-ounce popsicle molds with mixture. Freeze until partially set, 1½ to 2 hours.

2. Fill pop molds to top with orange juice. Cover molds with tops. Freeze until solid.

3. To remove pops, run hot water over the pop molds for 30 seconds to 1 minute. Pull pops from molds.

Frozen Fruit Pops

Use a variety of fruit, such as berries, peaches, and/or kiwis. If you don't have pop molds, you can use plastic cups and wooden pop sticks instead.

PREP TIME: 10 MINUTES • FREEZE TIME: 5 HOURS • MAKES: 8 SERVINGS

1 cup finely diced fresh fruit
½ cup plain or pink lemonade
    concentrate
1 cup water

1. Fill each of eight 2-ounce ice-pop molds or 7-ounce plastic cups with about 2 tablespoons diced fruit (molds should be half full).

2. Mix lemonade concentrate with water. Pour into molds and cover molds with tops. (If using cups, freeze 1½ hours, then place a pop stick upright in each cup.) Freeze until solid, at least 5 hours. To serve, run molds under warm water for 30 seconds to 1 minute and pop out.

VARIATION

Substitute cranberry (or another flavor) juice concentrate for the lemonade.

Cakes For All, Big and Small

Date-Nut-Ginger Cake

This lovely snack cake is just right for afternoon tea, or wrapped up in a lunchbox.

PREP TIME: 15 MINUTES • COOK TIME: 35 MINUTES • MAKES: 8 SERVINGS

1 package (14 ounces) gingerbread
    cookie and cake mix
1 cup water
1 cup chopped dates
⅔ cup chopped walnuts

1. Heat the oven to 350°F. Prepare gingerbread mix according to package directions, using water. Stir in dates and walnuts. Spoon mixture into a greased and floured 6-cup Bundt pan.

2. Bake until top springs back lightly when touched, 35 to 40 minutes. Cool completely in pan on a wire rack.

Perfect Party Cake

Why is the perfect party cake square? It's so much easier to cut.

PREP TIME: 30 MINUTES • COOK TIME: 35 MINUTES • MAKES: 12 SERVINGS

1 box (18.5 ounces) golden cake mix
1 stick (½ cup) butter, softened
⅔ cup water
3 eggs
⅔ cup seedless raspberry jam
½ cup lemon curd
3 cups marshmallow creme

1. Heat oven to 350°F. Prepare batter according to package directions, using the butter, water, and eggs. Spread batter in 2 greased and floured 8-inch-square baking pans.

2. Bake until a toothpick inserted in center comes out clean, about 35 minutes. Cool in the pans 10 minutes, then turn out on a wire rack and cool completely.

3. Cut each cake layer horizontally into 2 layers. Spread one layer with ⅓ cup raspberry jam. Top with a second cake layer and spread with all the lemon curd. Top with next layer and spread with remaining ⅓ cup raspberry jam. Top with remaining cake layer.

4. Refrigerate cake to firm up, about 1 hour. Spread top and sides of cake with marshmallow creme. Let stand at least 1 hour before serving.

Triple Orange-Apricot Cake

This is a very simple, fresh-tasting cake for the times when you don't want anything too fancy.

PREP TIME: 20 MINUTES • COOK TIME: 60 MINUTES • MAKES: 16 SERVINGS

1 package (6 ounces) Pacific-style
   dried apricots, finely chopped
2¼ cups orange juice
1 box (18.25 ounces) golden cake mix
1 stick (½ cup) butter, melted
3 eggs
1½ cups confectioners' sugar

1. Heat oven to 350°F. Combine the apricots and 1⅓ cups of the orange juice in a small saucepan. Heat to boiling, reduce the heat, and simmer until apricots are tender and liquid is evaporated, about 20 minutes. Cool to room temperature.

2. In a medium bowl, combine cake mix, using butter, eggs, and ⅔ cup of the orange juice. Beat with an electric mixer on medium speed until blended, about 4 minutes. Stir in the apricot mixture. Spread the batter in a greased and floured 13 x 9-inch baking pan.

3. Bake until a toothpick inserted in the center comes out clean, about 40 minutes. Stir together the sugar and the remaining ¼ cup orange juice. Poke holes all over the hot cake with a wooden skewer or toothpick and spread with the orange glaze mixture. Cool completely in pan on a wire rack.

Orange Marmalade Cake

This is a great party cake. It's beautiful and delicious.

PREP TIME: 25 MINUTES • COOK TIME: 23 MINUTES • MAKES: 12 TO 16 SERVINGS

1 box (18.5 ounces) golden cake mix
1 stick (½ cup) butter, softened
⅔ cup water
3 eggs
1 tub (16 ounces) vanilla frosting
1 cup orange marmalade

1. Heat the oven to 350°F. Prepare cake mix according to package directions, using the butter, water, and eggs. Divide the batter between 2 greased and floured 9-inch round cake pans.

2. Bake for 28 minutes or until a toothpick inserted in the center of each cake comes out clean. Cool in the pans for 10 minutes, then invert on wire rack and cool to room temperature.

3. Cut layers in half horizontally. Spread 2 tablespoons of the vanilla frosting over one layer, then spread with ¼ cup of the orange marmalade. Top with two more layers, spreading frosting and marmalade between each.

4. Spread the sides of the cake with remaining frosting, allowing the frosting to form a rim on the top of the cake. Fill the top with the remaining marmalade.

Banana Oatmeal Chip Cake

This yummy cake has everyone's favorite cake and cookie flavors: bananas, chocolate, nuts, and oatmeal. Who wouldn't love it?

PREP TIME: 10 MINUTES • COOK TIME: 25 MINUTES • MAKES: 16 SERVINGS

1 package (1 pound 1.5 ounces)
    oatmeal cookie mix
2 ripe bananas, mashed
⅓ cup vegetable oil
1 egg
½ cup chopped walnuts
½ cup chocolate chips

1. Heat the oven to 375°F. In a large bowl, combine oatmeal cookie mix, bananas, oil, and egg. Mix well. Stir in walnuts and chocolate chips. Spread batter into a foil-lined and lightly greased 9-inch-square baking pan.

2. Bake until golden, 35 to 40 minutes. Cool completely in pan on a wire rack, remove foil, and cut into squares.

Brownie Pudding Cake

This decadent cake is fudgy, rich, and oh-so-delicious. Try serving it with a dollop of whipped cream or crème fraîche.

PREP TIME: 15 MINUTES • COOK TIME: 1 HOUR • MAKES: 8 SERVINGS

1 package (21 ounces) chewy fudge brownie mix

1 cup water

½ cup vegetable oil

3 large eggs

½ cup prepared chocolate pudding

⅓ cup semisweet chocolate chips

3 tablespoons unsweetened cocoa powder

Confectioners' sugar, for dusting

1. Heat the oven to 350°F. In a medium bowl, combine the brownie mix, water, vegetable oil, eggs, pudding, chocolate chips, and cocoa powder. Stir until well blended. Spoon mixture into a greased and floured 9½-inch springform pan.

2. Bake 1 hour. Cool completely in pan on a wire rack. Just before serving, dust top of cake with confectioners' sugar.

Chocolate-Mint Layer Cake

Like a giant peppermint patty, this fun cake is minty, chocolatey, and yummy.

PREP TIME: 30 MINUTES • COOK TIME: 30 MINUTES • MAKES: 12 SERVINGS

1 package (1 pound 2.25 ounces)
   devil's food cake mix

1 ⅓ cups water

½ cup vegetable oil

3 eggs

6 tablespoons heavy cream

¾ teaspoon peppermint extract

3 cups confectioners' sugar

1 container (16 ounces) chocolate
   frosting

1. Heat oven to 350°F. Prepare cake mix according to package directions, using water, oil, and eggs, and divide the batter between 2 greased and floured 9-inch-round cake pans.

2. Bake for 30 minutes, or until a toothpick inserted in the center of each cake comes out clean. Cool in pans for 10 minutes, then turn out onto a wire rack and allow to cool completely.

3. In a large bowl, combine cream and mint extract. Sift the sugar into the bowl. Beat with a hand mixer 3 minutes on medium speed.

4. Spread all the mint filling on one cake layer to about ½ inch from the edge. Top with the second cake layer and refrigerate until firm, about 1 hour. Frost the sides, then the top of the cake with chocolate frosting.

Super Carrot Cake

This light carrot cake is simple to make and a delight to eat.

PREP TIME: 15 MINUTES • COOK TIME: 35 MINUTES • MAKES: 12 TO 14 SERVINGS

1 package (18.25 ounces) golden cake
mix
1 stick (½ cup) butter
⅔ cup orange juice
3 eggs
4 carrots, peeled and shredded
1 cup chopped walnuts
½ cup raisins
1 teaspoon pumpkin pie spice
1 container (16 ounces) cream cheese
frosting

1. Heat the oven to 350°F. Prepare cake mix according to package directions, using butter, orange juice instead of the water, and eggs. Stir in carrots, walnuts, raisins, and pumpkin pie spice. Spoon batter into a greased and floured 13 x 9-inch baking pan.

2. Bake about 35 minutes, or until a toothpick inserted in the center comes out clean. Cool completely in pan on a wire rack. Spread top of cake with frosting.

English Cherry Pound Cake

This simple pound cake is an English classic. Perfect for teatime.

PREP TIME: 10 MINUTES • COOK TIME: 55 MINUTES • MAKES: 8 TO 10 SERVINGS

⅓ cup almond paste, crumbled

¼ cup (½ stick) butter, softened

2 eggs

1 package (16 ounces) pound cake
   mix

⅔ cup milk

¾ cup glacéed cherries

½ cup currants

1. Heat the oven to 350°F. In a large bowl, combine almond paste and butter. Beat with an electric mixer on medium speed until smooth, 2 minutes. Beat in eggs, then cake mix and milk. Continue beating until thick and light, about 3 minutes. Stir in cherries and currants. Spoon mixture into a greased 9 x 5-inch loaf pan.

2. Bake until a toothpick inserted just off center of the cake comes out clean, 55 to 60 minutes. Cool completely in pan on a wire rack.

Banana Coconut Cake

If you prefer not to make frosting, use prepared vanilla or cream cheese frosting instead.

PREP TIME: 25 MINUTES • COOK TIME: 35 MINUTES • MAKES: 18 SERVINGS

1 package (18.25 ounces) golden cake
    mix
2 ripe bananas, mashed
2 sticks (1 cup) butter, softened
⅓ cup water
3 eggs
1 cup finely diced walnuts
2 cups sweetened flaked coconut
3½ cups confectioners' sugar
2 tablespoons milk

1. Heat the oven to 350°F. In a large bowl, combine cake mix, bananas, 1 stick of the butter, water, and eggs. With an electric mixer on medium speed, beat 4 minutes. Stir in 1 cup of the coconut and ¾ cup of the walnuts. Pour batter into a greased and floured 13 x 9-inch baking pan.

2. Bake until a toothpick inserted in the center comes out clean, about 35 minutes. Cool on a wire rack.

3. In a medium bowl, combine confectioners' sugar, milk, and the remaining stick of butter. Beat with an electric mixer on medium speed until light and fluffy. Stir in remaining 1 cup coconut. Frost top of cake. Sprinkle with the remaining ¼ cup walnuts.

Raspberry Chocolate Roulade

Rolling the cake when it's fresh from the oven is the best way to keep it from cracking.

PREP TIME: 30 MINUTES • COOK TIME: 22 MINUTES • MAKES: 10 TO 12 SERVINGS

1 box (16 ounces) angel food cake mix
1¼ cups water
⅓ cup cocoa powder
¼ cup confectioners' sugar, plus
  additional for dusting
1 cup heavy cream
⅓ cup sour cream
2 cups fresh raspberries

1. Heat the oven to 350°F. Line an 18 x 11 x 1-inch jelly roll pan with aluminum foil. Prepare cake mix according to package directions, using water. Add cocoa and beat just enough to blend. Spread evenly into prepared pan.

2. Bake until set, 22 minutes. Invert cake immediately onto a clean, lint-free dish towel dusted with confectioners' sugar. Remove foil carefully. Roll up cake with the towel jelly-roll fashion, starting at a long end. Cool completely.

3. In a large bowl, beat the heavy cream, sour cream, and ¼ cup confectioners' sugar with an electric mixer on medium speed until stiff peaks form. Unroll the cake and peel off towel. Spread with cream mixture and sprinkle with raspberries. Reroll and place, seam-side down, on a serving plate. Refrigerate at least 4 hours. Dust with additional confectioners' sugar before serving.

Chocolate Chip Cheesecake

This may be the most decadent cheesecake ever!

PREP TIME: 20 MINUTES • COOK TIME: 50 MINUTES • MAKES: 16 SERVINGS

1 roll (18 ounces) refrigerated
    chocolate chip cookie dough
24 ounces cream cheese, softened
¾ cup sugar
½ cup sour cream
2 eggs
2 teaspoons vanilla extract
1 tablespoon flour
½ cup mini chocolate chips

1. Heat the oven to 350°F. Unwrap cookie dough and press into bottom and sides of a greased 9-inch springform pan.

2. In a large bowl, beat the cream cheese, sugar, sour cream, eggs, vanilla, and flour until smooth. Fold in chocolate chips and pour into pan.

3. Bake until edges are firm but center is soft, 45 to 50 minutes. Cool completely in pan on a wire rack. Refrigerate at least 2 hours before serving.

Giant Berry Peach Shortcake

If you have fresh fruit on hand, go ahead and use it instead of the frozen. You will need about 4 cups of sliced peaches.

PREP TIME: 25 MINUTES • COOK TIME: 28 MINUTES • MAKES: 6 TO 8 SERVINGS

2⅓ cups baking mix
2 cups heavy cream
¾ cup sugar
2 cups frozen raspberries, thawed
1 package (16 ounces) frozen peach
    slices, thawed

1. Heat the oven to 425°F. In a large bowl, combine baking mix, ⅔ cup of the cream, and ¼ cup of the sugar. On a baking sheet, pat dough out to a 7-inch circle. Bake until dark golden, about 28 minutes. Let cool on pan 10 minutes, then transfer to a wire rack to cool completely.

2. Meanwhile, in a medium bowl, combine the raspberries, peaches, and remaining ½ cup sugar; toss. In a separate medium bowl, whip the remaining 1⅓ cups cream with an electric mixer on medium speed until stiff peaks form.

3. Slice the cooled shortcake in half. Place the bottom on a serving plate and top with the fruits and their juices, then the whipped cream, and then the top of the cake. Serve immediately.

Caramel-Pecan Cheesecake

There couldn't be an easier way to transform a prepared cheesecake into something extra special.

PREP TIME: 50 MINUTES • MAKES: 4 TO 6 SERVINGS

1 prepared (17 ounces) frozen
   cheesecake
3 tablespoons caramel ice cream
   topping
3 tablespoons chopped pecans

1. Defrost cheesecake according to package directions.

2. Drizzle cake with caramel sauce and sprinkle with nuts.

VARIATION

Chocolate-Pecan Cheesecake
Substitute chocolate or hot fudge ice cream topping for caramel ice cream topping.

Blueberry Pecan Upside-Down Cake

This great cake is perfect when blueberries are in season. And when they are not, you can use frozen berries—just defrost them first.

PREP TIME: 20 MINUTES • COOK TIME: 55 MINUTES • MAKES: 16 SERVINGS

2 cups blueberries

3 tablespoons sugar

1 package (1 pound 2.25 ounces)
   French vanilla cake mix

⅓ cup vegetable oil

3 eggs

1¼ cups orange juice

1 cup finely chopped pecans

1. Heat the oven to 350°F. Sprinkle blueberries and sugar into each of two 8-inch-round cake pans. Prepare cake batter according to package directions, using the oil and eggs and substituting orange juice for water. Stir in pecans. Divide batter between pans.

2. Bake until a toothpick inserted in the center of each cake comes out clean, 55 to 60 minutes. Let cakes cool in pans for 15 minutes. Place serving plates upside down over pans. Holding plates on top of pans, flip pans over and remove.

Lemon Cloud Cake

A lemon lover's dream, this cake is light, pretty, and delicious.

PREP TIME: 25 MINUTES • COOK TIME: 28 MINUTES • MAKES: 12 SERVINGS

1 package (1 pound 2.25 ounces)
  lemon cake mix
1/3 cup vegetable oil
3 eggs
1 1/3 cups water
2 1/2 cups heavy cream
7/8 cup lemon curd

1. Heat oven to 350°F. Prepare cake mix according to package directions, using oil, eggs, and water. Divide batter between 2 greased and floured 9-inch-round cake pans.

2. Bake for 28 minutes, or until a toothpick inserted in the center of each cake comes out clean. Cool in pans for 10 minutes, then turn out on a wire rack and cool to room temperature. Cut each cake in half horizontally.

3. In a large bowl, beat heavy cream and 1/2 cup of the lemon curd until stiff peaks form. Place one cake layer on a serving plate. Spread cake with 2 tablespoons of the remaining lemon curd, then top with 1 cup whipped cream mixture. Repeat twice, ending with cake. Cover the sides, then the top of cake with additional whipped cream. Refrigerate before serving.

VARIATION

Citrus Cloud Cake
Substitute orange curd for the lemon.

Banana Boston Cream Pie

This classic cake has gone bananas!

PREP TIME: 25 MINUTES • COOK TIME: 28 MINUTES • MAKES: 10 SERVINGS

1 package (1 pound 2.25 ounces)
    golden cake mix
1 stick (½ cup) butter, softened
⅔ cup water
3 eggs
2 ripe bananas, peeled and sliced
1½ cups vanilla pudding
1 cup semisweet chocolate chips
½ cup heavy cream

1. Heat the oven to 350°F. Prepare cake mix according to package directions, using the butter, water, and eggs. Divide the batter between 2 greased and floured 9-inch-round cake pans.

2. Bake for 28 minutes, or until a toothpick inserted in the center of each cake comes out clean. Cool in pans for 10 minutes, then turn out on a wire rack and cool to room temperature.

3. Arrange sliced bananas over the top of one cake layer. Spread with pudding almost to the edges of the cake. Top with the second layer, top-side up.

4. Place the chocolate chips in a small bowl. Heat the cream in a small saucepan over medium heat until almost boiling. Pour over the chocolate and stir until smooth. Drizzle the chocolate mixture over the cake, letting it run over the edges and down the sides of the cake layers. Refrigerate until ready to serve.

Ginger Refrigerator Cake

Think cookies and cream . . . with a ginger twist!

PREP TIME: 25 MINUTES • **MAKES: 8 SERVINGS**

2 cups heavy cream
2 tablespoons finely chopped
   crystallized ginger
51 gingersnaps

1. In a medium bowl, combine cream and crystallized ginger. Using an electric mixer, whip cream until stiff peaks form.

2. Line a 9-inch-round cake pan with a sheet of plastic wrap that overhangs the edges by 5 or 6 inches. Spread ¾ cup of the whipped cream to cover the bottom of the pan. Arrange 12 gingersnaps in a single layer over the cream (you might need to break an edge off the last cookie).

3. Spread ¾ cup of the cream over the cookies. Repeat layering with remaining cookies and cream, ending with cream.

4. Refrigerate, covered, until cookies are softened, 8 hours or overnight. Uncover, invert onto a serving plate, and gently pull the edges of the plastic wrap to release the cake. In a food processor, grind the remaining 3 cookies to make crumbs. Sprinkle crumbs over the cake and serve.

Coffee Cookie Cake

This is an update of the classic refrigerator cake.

PREP TIME: 25 MINUTES • **CHILL TIME: 4 HOURS** • **MAKES: 12 SERVINGS**

2 cups heavy cream
3 tablespoons confectioners' sugar
2 teaspoons instant coffee granules
36 chocolate wafer cookies

1. In a large bowl, combine cream, sugar, and coffee granules. Using an electric mixer, whip mixture until stiff peaks form.

2. Spread a thick layer of whipped cream on one side of a cookie and, standing cookies on end, gently press a second cookie against the cream. Spread whipped cream on the unfrosted side of the second cookie and press the third cookie against the second.

3. Continue layering with whipped cream and cookies until you have a long row of 18 cookies. Carefully transfer the row of cookies to a large flat tray. Repeat with the other 18 cookies and cream and lay them next to the first row. Spread the remaining whipped cream to cover the entire surface. Refrigerate until firm, about 4 hours.

Raspberry Tea Cake

This simple tea cake takes just minutes to make but impresses like you won't believe.

PREP TIME: 15 MINUTES • MAKES: 12 SERVINGS

1 prepared all-butter loaf cake
   (12 ounces)
½ cup seedless raspberry jam

1. Cut loaf cake horizontally into 5 layers. Spread bottom layer evenly with 2 tablespoons of the jam. Top with next cake layer. Repeat with remaining layers, rebuilding the cake.

2. Wrap cake in plastic wrap and refrigerate until firm, about 2 hours. Slice before serving.

VARIATION

Lemon or Orange Tea Cake
Substitute lemon or orange curd for the raspberry jam.

Caramel-Nut Cake

A decadent combination and a beautiful cake.

PREP TIME: 25 MINUTES • COOK TIME: 35 MINUTES • MAKES: 2 CAKES, 16 SERVINGS

1 package (18.25 ounces) French
    vanilla cake mix

1¼ cups water

⅓ cup vegetable oil

3 eggs

2 cups very finely chopped pecans

1 jar (11.5 ounces) dulce de leche

2 cups confectioners' sugar

½ stick (¼ cup) butter, softened

Pecan halves, for garnish

1. Heat the oven to 350°F. Prepare batter according to package directions, using water, oil, and eggs. Stir in the chopped nuts. Spoon into 2 greased and floured 8-inch-round baking pans.

2. Bake about 35 minutes until a toothpick inserted in center comes out clean. Cool in pans for 10 minutes, then invert cakes and cool completely on a wire rack.

3. While cakes are cooling, make the icing. In a large bowl, stir together the dulce de leche, confectioners' sugar, and butter until blended. Spoon onto top of cakes. Gently spread icing to edges and allow it to drip over the sides, then spread icing over sides. Decorate tops of cakes with pecan halves. Set aside until icing is dry, 1 to 2 hours.

Black-and-White Ice Cream Cake

This great no-bake cake is perfect for kids and grown-ups alike.

PREP TIME: 15 MINUTES • FREEZE TIME: 8 HOURS • MAKES: 16 SERVINGS

1 prepared 8-inch angel food cake
(keep plastic cake container)
4½ cups chocolate ice cream, slightly
softened

1. Slice the angel food cake horizontally into 4 slices. Place the top layer back into the plastic container. Spread evenly with 1½ cups of the ice cream (you might need to use your fingers for this). Top with the next layer and repeat twice with ice cream and cake layers, rebuilding the cake. Top with remaining cake layer.

2. Cover container with plastic wrap and freeze until very firm, about 8 hours. Slice into wedges before serving.

Mini Ginger Cheesecakes

These cute little cheesecakes have the great grown-up flavor of ginger. If you prefer, you can top them with apricot jam or orange marmalade instead.

PREP TIME: 20 MINUTES • COOK TIME: 20 MINUTES • MAKES: 12

16 ounces cream cheese, softened
½ cup sugar
2 eggs
½ teaspoon vanilla extract
12 gingersnap cookies
2 tablespoons ginger marmalade

1. Heat oven to 350°F. In a large bowl, beat cream cheese, sugar, eggs, and vanilla with an electric mixer on medium speed until smooth.

2. Place 1 gingersnap cookie in each of 12 paper-lined muffin cups. Pour batter into cups, dividing evenly.

3. Bake until firm, 20 to 22 minutes. Cool on pan. Warm marmalade in microwave until syrupy. Spread over cakes and refrigerate 1 hour. Remove paper cups from cakes before serving.

Chocolate Cheesecake Cupcakes

Not just cream cheese frosting but a cheesecake surprise inside!

PREP TIME: 25 MINUTES • COOK TIME: 24 MINUTES • MAKES: 24

1 package (1 pound 2.25 ounces)
    devil's food cake mix
⅔ cup water
½ cup vegetable oil
3 eggs
20 ounces cream cheese, softened
½ cup granulated sugar
2 tablespoons flour
1 stick (½ cup) butter, softened
1 cup confectioners' sugar

1. Heat the oven to 350°F. Prepare cake mix according to package directions, using the water, oil, and eggs. Spoon into 24 paper-lined muffin cups.

2. In a medium bowl, combine 12 ounces of the cream cheese, the granulated sugar, and the flour. Beat until smooth. Dollop 1½ tablespoons of the mixture into each batter-filled cup. Bake until a toothpick inserted in the center comes out clean, 20 to 24 minutes. Cool completely on a wire rack before frosting.

3. To make frosting, in a medium bowl, beat the remaining 8 ounces of cream cheese with the butter and confectioners' sugar until light. Refrigerate just until spreadable. Spread over tops of cupcakes.

Chocolate-Hazelnut Cupcakes

These delicious cupcakes have a sophisticated hazelnut flavor.

PREP TIME: 15 MINUTES • COOK TIME: 19 MINUTES • MAKES: 24

1 package (1 pound 2.25 ounces)
   devil's food cake mix
1 ⅓ cups water
½ cup vegetable oil
3 eggs
1 ½ cups finely chopped hazelnuts
¾ cup chocolate-hazelnut spread

1. Heat the oven to 350°F. Prepare cake mix according to package directions, using the water, oil, and eggs. Stir 1 cup of the nuts into batter. Spoon into 24 paper-lined muffin cups. Bake until a toothpick inserted in the center comes out clean, 19 to 23 minutes. Cool completely in pan on a wire rack.

2. Spread cupcakes with chocolate hazelnut spread and sprinkle with remaining nuts.

Mini Mocha Brownie Cakes

These little chocolate cakes are for coffee lovers only.

PREP TIME: 20 MINUTES • **COOK TIME: 30 MINUTES** • **MAKES: 12 SERVINGS**

4 teaspoons instant coffee granules
¼ cup water
1 package (21 ounces) chewy fudge
    brownie mix
½ cup vegetable oil
3 eggs
¾ cup semisweet chocolate chips
½ cup heavy cream

1. Heat the oven to 350°F. Dissolve 2 teaspoons of the instant coffee granules into the ¼ cup water. Prepare brownie mix according to package directions, using the water, oil, and eggs.

2. Spoon the batter into 12 paper-lined muffin cups and bake until a toothpick inserted into the center of a cake comes out clean, 25 to 30 minutes. Cool in pan on a wire rack.

3. Place chocolate chips in a small bowl. In a small saucepan, heat cream and the remaining 2 teaspoons coffee granules until almost boiling. Pour cream over the chocolate chips and stir until melted. Refrigerate until spreadable, stirring occasionally, about 1 hour. Stir chocolate mixture until smooth before spreading on cakes.

Little Lemon Cakes

These great little glazed cakes have just the perfect bite of lemony sweetness.

PREP TIME: 15 MINUTES • COOK TIME: 18 MINUTES • MAKES: 24 CAKES

1 box (18.25 ounces) golden cake mix
1 stick (½ cup) butter, melted
⅔ cup water
3 eggs
1 tablespoon grated lemon zest
2 cups confectioners' sugar
⅔ cup lemon juice

1. Heat oven to 350°F. Prepare the cake mix according to package directions, using the butter, water, and eggs. Stir in lemon zest. Spoon into 24 greased extra-large muffin cups and bake until just golden, 18 to 20 minutes.

2. Poke holes all over the warm cakes with a fork. In a medium bowl, whisk together confectioners' sugar and lemon juice. Drizzle over the cakes. Cool completely in pan on a wire rack.

Coconut Cream Cupcakes

These pretty fluffy white cupcakes are a classic coconut lover's treat.

PREP TIME: 15 MINUTES • COOK TIME: 21 MINUTES • MAKES: 24 CUPCAKES

1 box (18.5 ounces) white cake mix
1⅓ cups water
3 large egg whites
2 tablespoons vegetable oil
2½ cups sweetened flaked coconut
1½ cups heavy cream

1. Prepare cake mix according to package directions, using the water, egg whites, and vegetable oil. Stir 1 cup of the flaked coconut into the batter. Spoon batter into 24 paper-lined muffin cups. Bake until a toothpick inserted in the center comes out clean, 21 to 24 minutes. Cool on a wire rack.

2. In a large bowl, whip the cream to stiff peaks. Top each cupcake with 2 tablespoons whipped cream, and sprinkle with the remaining flaked coconut. Serve right away or refrigerate until ready to serve.

Very Berry Snack Cake

This easy fruit-topped cake is perfect for a sweet bite in the afternoon. You can use any berries you like.

PREP TIME: 10 MINUTES • COOK TIME: 45 MINUTES • MAKES: 16 SERVINGS

1 roll (18 ounces) refrigerated sugar cookie dough
1 package (12 ounces) frozen mixed berries, thawed
2 tablespoons sugar
2 teaspoons cornstarch

1. Heat the oven to 350°F. Crumble three-fourths of the cookie dough into a foil-lined 9-inch-square baking pan. Using your fingers, press it evenly into the bottom to form a thick crust.

2. Cut the strawberries from the mixed berries in half. In a medium bowl, toss the berries with sugar and cornstarch. Sprinkle the berry mixture evenly over the dough. Crumble the remaining dough over the berries.

3. Bake until golden, about 45 minutes. Cool completely in pan on a wire rack and cut into 16 squares.

Apricot-Date Nut Muffins

These muffins are perfect for brunches.

PREP TIME: 15 MINUTES • **COOK TIME: 20 MINUTES** • **MAKES: 12**

1 package (16.6 ounces) date quick
   bread and muffin mix
¼ cup vegetable oil
2 eggs
1 cup apricot nectar
¼ teaspoon almond extract
½ cup apricot preserves
½ cup sliced almonds

1. Heat the oven to 400°F. Grease a 12-cup muffin pan. Prepare muffin mix according to package directions, using the oil and eggs, substituting apricot nectar for the milk. Stir in almond extract.

2. Fill muffin cups almost half full. Place 2 teaspoons apricot preserves on top of the batter in the center of each cup. Top with the remaining batter. Sprinkle with sliced almonds.

3. Bake until golden, about 20 minutes. Cool completely in pan on a wire rack.

Chocolate Babka Buns

A traditional babka takes more than two hours to prepare. You can enjoy this version much sooner.

PREP TIME: 20 MINUTES • COOK TIME: 18 MINUTES • MAKES: 8 SERVINGS

3 tablespoons flour
5 tablespoons sugar
6 tablespoons (¾ stick) butter, melted
½ cup mini chocolate chips
¼ teaspoon ground cinnamon
1 can (12.4 ounces) cinnamon rolls

1. Heat the oven to 400°F. Combine the flour, 3 tablespoons of the sugar, and 2 tablespoons of the melted butter. Squeeze the mixture together with your fingertips to make large crumbs. In a separate small bowl, combine the chocolate chips, the remaining 2 tablespoons of sugar, and the cinnamon.

2. Open the cinnamon buns and, using a rolling pin, roll out each one to ⅛- to ¼-inch thickness. Sprinkle the coated side of each bun with crumbs and then with the chocolate chip mixture, dividing evenly. Fold each in half (like a taco) and place side by side in a greased 8-inch-square baking pan. Drizzle with remaining melted butter.

3. Bake until golden, 18 to 20 minutes. Cool on pan 10 minutes, then transfer to a wire rack to cool completely.